CONTENTS

RECIPE CREDITS

Recipes on pages 190, 191, 194, 197, 198, 200, 201, 207, 215, 216, 221, 225, 232, 234, 235, 238, 240, 243, 247, 248, 249, 255, 258, 263, 265, 266, 267, and 268 from *A-24 52 Great Green Tomato Recipes* by Phyllis Hobson, Garden Way Publishing, 1978.

Recipe on page 182 from *A-32 Jams, Jellies & Preserves* by Imogene McTague, Garden Way Publishing, 1980.

Recipes on pages 44 and 54 from *A-97 Salt-Free Herb Cookery* by Edith Stovel, Garden Way Publishing, 1985.

Recipe on page 97 from *A-105 Fast and Healthy Ways to Cook Vegetables* by Penny Noepel, Garden Way Publishing, 1988.

Recipe on page 43 from *A-106 Recipes for Gourmet Vegetables* by Glenn Andrews, Garden Way Publishing, 1988.

Recipes on pages 55, 70, 138, and 170 from *A-107 Cooking with Fresh Sausage* by Charles Reavis, Garden Way Publishing, 1988.

Recipes on pages 159 and 171 from *A-115 Cooking with Potatoes* by Dorothy Parker, Storey/Garden Way Publishing, 1990.

Recipe on page 178 from *It's the Berries!* by Liz Anton and Beth Dooley, Garden Way Publishing, 1988.

Recipes on pages 45, 75, 76, 77, 80, 92, and 258 from *Seasonal Salads* by David Scott and Paddy Byrne, Garden Way Publishing, 1986.

Recipes on pages 57, 155, and 158 from *The Carrot Cookbook* by Audra and Jack Hendrickson, Garden Way Publishing, 1986.

Recipes on pages 65, 139, 154, and 160 from *Glorious Garlic* by Charlene Braida, Garden Way Publishing, 1986.

Recipes on pages 64, 101, 137, 147, and 157 from *Corn, Meals & More* by Olwen Woodier, Garden Way Publishing, 1987.

Recipes on pages 34, 68, 74, 98, 125, 164, and 177 from *The Elegant Onion* by Betty Cavage, Garden Way Publishing, 1987.

Recipes on pages 35, 56, 62, 63, 69, and 148 from *The More Than Chicken Cookbook* by Sara Pitzer, Garden Way Publishing, 1984.

Recipes on pages 48, 67, 105, 109, and 113 from *Home Gardener's Month-by-Month Cookbook* by Marjorie Blanchard, Garden Way Publishing, 1974.

Recipes on pages 49, 50, 60, 66, 131, 134, 136, 140, 144, 146, 150, 152, 153, and 174 from *The Easy Harvest Sauce & Puree Cookbook* by Marjorie Blanchard, Garden Way Publishing, 1980.

Recipes on pages 99, 127, 128, 129, 130, 132, 133, 135, 151, 156, 161, 163, 167, 168, and 169 from *The Power of Pasta* by Olwen Woodier, Garden Way Publishing, 1985.

TOMATOES!

365 HEALTHY RECIPES for YEAR-ROUND ENJOYMENT

By the Editors of
Garden Way Publishing

A Garden Way Publishing Book

Storey Communications, Inc.
Schoolhouse Road
Pownal, Vermont 05261

Cover photograph by David Cavagnaro
Cover design by Judy Eliason
Text design and production by Judy Eliason
Drawings by Brigita Fuhrmann
Edited by Constance L. Oxley
Indexed by Kathleen D. Bagioni

The name Garden Way Publishing is licensed to Storey Communications, Inc. by Garden Way, Inc.

Printed in the United States by Haddon Craftsmen, Inc.
First printing May 1991

Library of Congress Cataloging-in-Publication Data

Tomatoes! : 365 healthy recipes for year-round enjoyment / by the editors of Garden Way Publishing.
p. cm.
Includes index.
ISBN 0-88266-673-8 (hc) — ISBN 0-88266-672-X (pb)
1. Cookery (Tomatoes) I. Garden Way Publishing.
TX803.T6T66 1991
641.6'5642—dc20

90-55864
CIP

Introduction

Picture yourself in a summer garden with delicious tomatoes hanging in clusters of red and green, promising succulent delight. Pluck one of those ripe tomatoes, smooth and silky to the touch, and let the sweet warm flavor of summer explode in your mouth. This is one way to enjoy a tomato. Another way is to stop by your local farmer's roadside stand or your favorite mom & pop market and buy a bag of fresh, juicy, vine-ripened tomatoes.

There are countless ways to appreciate the rich, juicy goodness of tomatoes. This is a book about enjoying the taste you associate with the joys of summer — all year long.

The tomato is the most popularly grown vegetable in North America for a number of reasons. First, it's one of the tastiest vegetables around. Also, it's a very nutritious food, ranking high in vitamins A and C and potassium. As you can see from all the recipes collected here, the tomato is a very versatile food — there really is no such thing as too many tomatoes.

1

Terrific Tomato Ideas

Quick Dinners

If you're a cook who likes helpful hints for menu planning, but really enjoys a free rein to create your meals, this section is for you. Here are some food combination ideas to help you plan easy, tomato-based side dishes, sauces, and casseroles, by combining, mixing, and matching certain foods and herbs.

For side dishes, sauté tomatoes with any one or a combination of vegetables and flavor with an herb or spice or a combination of both, such as the ones suggested on pages 7 and 8.

To make a tomato-based casserole, layer the sauce with vegetables, grains, or pasta and finish with a cheese and crumb topping. Bake for 30-60 minutes.

Vegetables to combine with tomatoes:

Green cabbage	Zucchini	Lima beans
Corn	Broccoli	Chick-peas
Peas	Cauliflower	Black olives
Mushrooms	Onions	Celery
Eggplant	Green bell peppers	Okra

Cooked meats and fish to mix in:

Chicken	Ham	Shrimp
Turkey	Lean sausage, *hot or sweet*	Clams
Lean ground lamb	Lean ground pork	Tuna
Lean lamb, *cubed*	Lean pork, *cubed*	Salmon
Lean ground beef	Lean bacon	Red snapper
Lean beef, *cubed*	Fillets of sole, bass, or turbot	Mussels

Liquids for flavor:

Wine	Beef broth	Low-fat sour cream
Vegetable broth	Prepared mustard	Half-and-half
Chicken broth	Tomato sauce	

Cheeses to match:

Parmesan	Swiss	Blue cheese
Low-fat cheddar	Low-fat mozzarella	Feta

Serve on:

Pasta of any shape	White rice	Cooked leaf spinach
Couscous	Polenta	Toast
Brown rice	Spaghetti squash	

Top with:

Sesame seeds	Wheat germ	Cracker crumbs
	Bread crumbs	

Salad Combos

Any of these salad combinations are great with sliced, diced, or quartered tomatoes. Slice, dice, or chop the vegetables. Mix with the tomatoes and top with a simple vinaigrette dressing.

Mexican

Avocados
Red bell peppers
Chick-peas
Cooked corn
Green bell peppers

Farm-style

Carrots
Green bell peppers
Cucumbers
Kohlrabi

French

Mushrooms
Parsley
Peas

Oriental

Broccoli (blanched)
Water chestnuts
Soy sauce or tamari
Cashews

Greek

Black olives
Feta cheese
Red onions
Dill
Green bell peppers

Herb & Spice Combinations

Whether you are throwing together a quick casserole or creating a new tomato dish from scratch, you can use these dried herb and ground spice combinations to achieve special, authentic tastes.

Mexican

Chile powder
Cumin
Garlic
Onion
Hot chile peppers
Coriander leaves or cilantro

Southern French

Onion
Garlic
Thyme
Basil
Bay leaf

French Canadian

Cinnamon
Sugar
Nutmeg

Indian

Curry powder
Hot chile peppers
Turmeric
Cumin

Oriental

Soy sauce or tamari
Five-Spice Powder (or anise, or fennel, or ginger)

Greek

Lemon	Parsley	Thyme
Garlic	Dill	

Northern French

Tarragon	Parsley	Onion

Italian

Onion	Thyme	Parsley
Garlic	Oregano	Marjoram
	Basil	

English

Sage

Celery seeds or mustard seeds

Russian

Caraway seeds

Dill

Creole

Horseradish	Lemon	Tabasco sauce

Creative Tomato Garnishes

Sometimes a special meal calls for some special touches. You can add a sprig of parsley to a serving platter, or sprinkle some chopped scallions on top of a dish. But tomatoes add the most distinctive touches to a meal. Sliced or wedged tomatoes encircling a platter add lovely color. Stuffed tomatoes are another great garnish for a serving platter, especially if you take the time to make a tomato crown or basket.

Here are some of the tomato garnishes used to transform ordinary meals into special "catered affairs."

TOMATO ROSE: The tomato rose is the supreme tomato garnish. It looks so realistic, it can compete with a rose straight from the garden. You can also use a large rose and a small rose together, cutting green bell peppers as leaves or setting the roses on a bed of watercress.

Tomato roses are not hard to make, but don't expect perfect results the first time. Increase your chances for success by sharpening a knife for the job, and always select firm, ripe tomatoes. The tomatoes should be medium in size.

A tomato rose is made from a continuous strip of tomato peel, cut ¾ inch wide. Experience will teach you how thick to make this strip. It should be thick enough so that it does not break, but not so thick that it won't bend.

1. Working from the stem end, insert the point of your tomato knife into the tomato to the depth you want for the peel. Slide the knife so that the edge of the blade is parallel to the surface of the skin.

2. Begin peeling around the tomato in a continuous strip. Be sure to hold the tomato near the working surface so the strip does not dangle and break. (If your strip breaks, you can still use it; more on that later.)

3. At the bottom of the tomato, the strip will end with a little curl that becomes the "hook" to hold your rose together. You are now ready to wrap your rose.

4. Take the beginning of the tomato strip and wrap it around your index finger. Continue wrapping the strip on top of itself until you reach the end.

5. Hook the tail into the previous ring, or petal. Slip the rose off your finger and, if necessary, tighten the center of the rose by turning the center of the spiral.

6. Invert the rose and position it on the serving platter.

If you have a few broken pieces, try this method. Take the longest piece and start rolling it with one edge against the working surface so you can see the top of the rose forming as you roll. Before you come to the end of the first piece, work in the second piece, and so on, until you have worked the last piece in. Hook the end of the last strip into the rose and move the rose carefully to the serving platter.

The roses can be stored in the refrigerator on a plate covered with a damp towel for a few hours.

TOMATO PEONY. Here's another tomato garnish that closely resembles a flower and it is easier to make than the rose. The peony is a rather large garnish and should be used on a large serving platter.

Hold a firm tomato stem side down. Starting on one side, make a cut across the top of the tomato three-quarters of the way through the tomato. Make a second cut, parallel to the first, about ¼ inch beyond. Continue making parallel cuts, each three-quarters of the way through, across the tomato, leaving ¼ inch between cuts. Turn the tomato a quarter turn, and make a second series of deep cuts ¼ inch apart across the tomato to create little squares. Gently spread the petals, being careful not to break any.

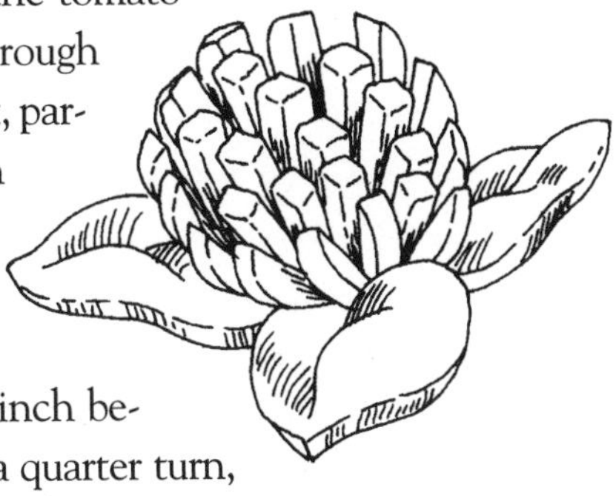

Cut two or three leaf shapes from a green bell pepper and place them around the blossom.

TOMATO BUTTERFLY. This garnish will delight children as well as adults. It is one of the best garnishes you can make with green tomatoes. Take a large firm red or green tomato and cut it into ¼-inch slices. Cut each slice in half and dip the cut edges into 2 tablespoons of minced parsley to coat them. Place the slices back-to-back on the dish you are decorating. Cut two small pieces of chives or scallion greens and place them on the tomato slices to make eyes. Arrange two longer pieces of chives to make antennae.

TOMATO ACCORDIAN. Eggs, cucumbers, or bell peppers can be used with this garnish, depending on what colors you wish to emphasize.

Remove a thin slice from the stem end of the tomato to make sure the tomato stands flat. Set the tomato on the cut end. Make five deep slits into the tomato. Slip slices of hard-boiled egg, cucumber, or bell pepper between the slits.

MUSHROOM BOWL. This garnish can be used with hot or cold foods. The mushrooms can be raw or lightly sautéed.

Remove the stem from the mushroom. Set the mushroom cut side up on a platter. Place a half cherry tomato inside the mushroom where the stem had been. Set three mushrooms together on a bed of parsley for a very unusual garnish on the side of your platter.

With a cold dish, you may want to garnish with zucchini or cucumber slices and halved cherry tomatoes, instead of mushrooms.

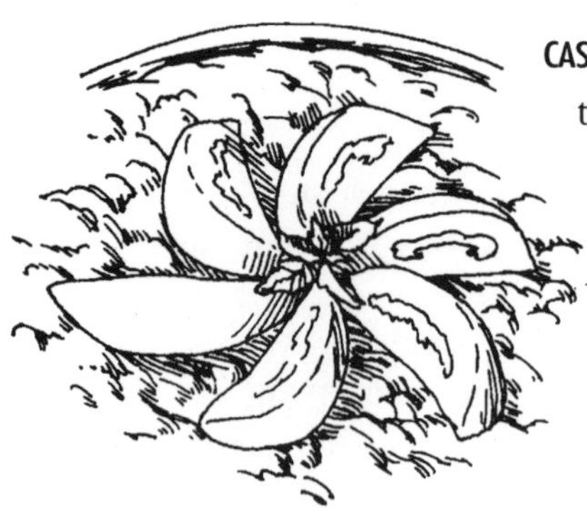

CASSEROLE GARNISH. Cut a tomato into wedges. Arrange the wedges in an overlapping circle at the center of any casserole dish during the last 20 minutes of baking time. For cold dishes, arrange the tomato wedges just before serving.

Surprising Stuffed Tomatoes

The ordinary garden tomato is transformed into something quite exotic when filled with a delicious savory filling. Everything from gourmet treats to leftovers can be presented in the natural serving bowl that a hollowed-out tomato becomes. Little stuffed cherry tomatoes make colorful, easily served hors d'oeuvres or appetizers. Full-sized tomatoes can be stuffed with salads or raw vegetables for a first course or light lunch, or they can be stuffed with meats and cooked vegetables as a main course.

Be sure that you work with a sharp paring knife. Since the stem end of the tomato is flatter, make that end the bottom and then the tomatoes will not roll off the plate. This is particularly important with cherry tomatoes. You can bake stuffed tomatoes in muffin cups to help them hold their shape and not roll over. All stuffed tomatoes can be peeled first to make them easier to eat, but tomatoes with skins are more nutritious.

Save the insides of the tomatoes! The pulp can be used in soups, stews, gravies, and salad dressings.

THE BASIC SHAPE. For a basic stuffed tomato, simply cut off the bottom of the tomato, scoop out the insides, drain, and stuff.

TOMATO BASKET. A whimsical change for stuffed tomatoes is the tomato basket. It is served filled with cold foods. Use only large firm tomatoes and an extra sharp, serrated knife.

1. Looking down at the top of the tomato (the stem end), slice into

the tomato just right of the stem scar. Draw your knife halfway down into the tomato, stop, and bring the knife back up.

Make another cut, parallel to the first on the other side of the stem scar, about ¾ inch from the first slice.

2. Now make two more cuts into the sides of the tomatoes so that these cuts meet the slices you made in Step 1.

3. Remove the wedges of tomato you just cut. What remains is the basket handle and basket.

4. Using your knife, remove the pulp and seeds from the handle. Leave as much of the flesh of the tomato as possible, so that the handle stays firm.

5. Remove as much seed and pulp as possible from the basket.

6. Stuff the basket with a cold salad. If you like, add a sprig of parsley as a "ribbon" decoration.

TOMATO BOWL. Use a tomato bowl instead of a porcelain bowl to serve relishes. A hollowed-out tomato can hold tiny pickled onions, olives, relishes, or sliced pickles on a sandwich plate or cold-cut plate for a picnic or buffet.

Select a large firm tomato. Remove the bottom of the tomato.

Scoop out the insides and allow the tomato to drain for a few minutes on a paper towel. Set the tomato on a platter, stem side down, and fill.

TOMATO CROWN. Here's a classic tomato shape that is good for hot and cold foods. Use a firm tomato of any size. The crown is made by a series of V-shaped cuts all the way around the tomato.

To start, hold the tomato in one hand and push your sharp paring knife into the tomato at a 45° angle, midway down the side of the tomato. Remove the knife. Now make another cut into the tomato at a 45° angle in the opposite direction. The bottom edge of the second cut should meet the bottom edge of the first cut so that a V is formed. Continue making these V-shaped cuts around the entire tomato. Pull the two halves apart and scoop out the insides. Fill each half with the stuffing of your choice. Or, fill the first half with your stuffing and top with the second half of the tomato.

To use a tomato crown as a garnish, fill the cups with sprigs of parsley and set the crowns on a serving platter filled with other foods.

TOMATO WHEEL. Tomato wheels are filled with cold foods and are easy to make. Holding the tomato with the stem side down, make a long diagonal cut from the near top of the tomato to halfway down its side. From the bottom edge of this cut, make a second cut up, in the opposite direction, to make a long V-shaped cut. Make a second V-shaped cut to match the first. Continue until you have made eight identical wedges (sixteen cuts). Remove the top of the tomato and

the wedges you have made. Scoop out a little of the center. This section can be filled with a cold stuffing, such as ham salad. Take thin slices of cheese and using a 1-1½-inch fluted cookie cutter, make eight rounds of cheese. Put a cheese circle in each wedge.

TOMATO BLOSSOM. You can use either peeled or unpeeled tomatoes for tomato blossoms. Serve hot or cold foods in the blossoms.

Turn the tomato stem end down and cut the tomato into seven petals that extend two-thirds of the way down the sides. Gently spread the petals out. Scoop out the flesh of the tomato and fill the center with the filling. Then close the petals up over the stuffing.

If you are planning to use a very liquid filling, cut the petals only one-third of the way down the tomato.

TOMATO SLICES. Here is another low-calorie alternative to bread for serving a cold salad.

Cut a large tomato into thick slices. Top each slice with a slightly smaller ring of green bell pepper. Spoon the filling into the green bell pepper ring and garnish.

STRIPED TOMATO. This tomato should be filled with a firm, cold salad. It makes a wonderful low-calorie alternative to a sandwich.

Cut each tomato into three thick slices and neatly spread the filling between the layers. Then carefully restack the layers.

BED DOWN THAT TOMATO!

For the best effect, serve your stuffed tomatoes on a beautiful dish. Make a bed for the tomatoes by arranging fresh, crisp lettuce leaves or shredded vegetables on the serving dish. Then set your tomatoes on top. Here are some suggestions:

Spinach	Parsley	Shredded cabbage
Watercress	Sprouts	Shredded carrots
	Swiss chard	

Be adventurous when you decorate your stuffed tomatoes. Make a green trim on the edge of your tomatoes by dipping the tomato in finely chopped fresh parsley. Or choose one of the following garnishes to sprinkle on top.

Fresh herbs:

Basil	Oregano	Mint
Sage	Dill	Chives

Seeds:

Sesame	Pumpkin	Poppy

Chopped Nuts:

Walnuts	Almonds	Cashews
	Hazelnuts	

Grated or diced vegetables:

Scallions	Green bell peppers	Pickles
Radishes	Beets	Capers
Carrots	Olives	

EGG SALAD STUFFINGS

Dress up your usual egg salad with any one of these ingredients to make a tasty luncheon dish. Stuff into tomato shells and serve on a bed of crisp lettuce.

CHINESE CHOICE: 2 tablespoons water chestnuts, minced.

SPRING SALAD: ¼ cup celery, minced with 1 teaspoon celery seed.

GARDEN SIDE: 2 tablespoons minced fresh parsley.

PICKLERS' PREFERENCE: 1 tablespoon dried dill. Garnish with cucumber slices.

BOMBAY-STYLE: 2 teaspoons curry powder.

GENOA EGGS: ¼ cup grated Parmesan cheese and 1 teaspoon dried basil.

PARISIAN: 1 tablespoon minced capers.

RUSSIAN APPROACH: 1½ teaspoons caraway seeds and 1 tablespoon minced pickles.

DEEP-SEA DIVER: 2 teaspoons anchovy paste, garnished with anchovy wheels (rolled up anchovy fillets).

WESTERN RANGE: 1 scallion, finely minced, and ¼ cup finely minced ham.

CHICKEN SALAD STUFFINGS

Take your favorite chicken salad recipe, add one of these variations, and stuff into tomato shells for an attractive light meal.

AVOCADO CURRY: Dice 1 avocado and add to the chicken salad, with 2 teaspoons curry powder, a squeeze of fresh lemon juice, and low-calorie mayonnaise.

CHICKEN WALDORF: Add diced apple, green grapes, walnuts, and low-calorie mayonnaise.

SUNSHINE SALAD: Add 1-2 tablespoons honey, 1 orange, divided into sections, 2 teaspoons poppy seeds, and low-calorie mayonnaise.

CHEESE STUFFINGS

Make a special cheese spread to stuff into a tomato cup.

FARM-STYLE: Combine low-fat cottage cheese with fresh chives, dried basil, dried dill, and scallions.

LIPTAUER: A traditional Austrian spread made by combining 1 cup low-fat cottage cheese, 2 tablespoons paprika, 1½ teaspoons caraway seeds, 1 scallion, minced, and 2-3 tablespoons Dijon mustard. Mix in a blender or food processor until smooth.

BLUE CHEESE: Combine low-fat cottage cheese with blue cheese and diced onions.

GREEK-STYLE: Combine low-fat cream cheese with feta cheese, fresh parsley, and dried dill.

COASTAL DELIGHT: Combine low-fat cream cheese with smoked oysters, fresh lemon juice, and Tabasco sauce.

HERO: Combine diced low-fat cheddar or Swiss cheese with raw diced vegetables and slices of pepperoni. Pour a vinaigrette dressing over the filling.

HOT VEGETABLE CUPS

Tomatoes make natural bowls or containers for garden vegetables. Hot vegetables should be blanched for 2-3 minutes, and then reheated in the tomato cups.

PEAS: Fill the cups and bake for 10 minutes.

BROCCOLI: Blanch broccoli florets. Place florets, stem first, in the cups. Dot with butter or soft margarine and bake for 5-10 minutes.

CAULIFLOWER: Blanch cauliflower pieces. Place in tomato cups. Melt

2 tablespoons butter or soft margarine and brown ½ cup bread crumbs. Sprinkle the crumbs over the cauliflower and bake for 10 minutes.

GREEN BEANS: Blanch beans. Garnish with almonds and bake for 10 minutes.

CORN: Fill the tomato cups with cooked whole kernel corn. Garnish with minced fresh parsley, chopped chives, and chopped red bell pepper.

MUSHROOMS: Sauté mushrooms and diced onions in butter or soft margarine. Reheat in tomato cups.

Hummus Stuffed Tomatoes

YIELD: 8-10 SERVINGS
TIME: 15 MINUTES

2 cups cooked chick-peas
2 cloves garlic, minced
3 tablespoons tahini (sesame seed paste)
¼ cup fresh lemon juice
Salt to taste
50 red cherry tomatoes, with insides scooped out

In a blender or food processor, mix all the ingredients, except the tomatoes. Blend until smooth. Stuff the mixture into the tomatoes. Serve the remaining *Hummus* with vegetable sticks or Syrian pita bread.

Tofu Tahini Salad Cups

YIELD: 4 SERVINGS
TIME: 25 MINUTES

3 tablespoons tamari or soy sauce

3 tablespoons water

1 clove garlic, minced

½ pound tofu, cut into small cubes

⅓ cup tahini (sesame seed paste)

2 tablespoons fresh lemon juice

4 firm, medium red tomatoes, with insides scooped out

In a large bowl, mix the tamari, water, and garlic together. Add the tofu and let stand for 15 minutes.

Remove the tofu. Add the tahini and lemon juice to the remaining liquid and mix well. Stir this liquid into the tofu. Stuff the mixture into the tomatoes and serve.

Mushroom Pecan Pâté

YIELD: 8-10 SERVINGS
TIME: 25 MINUTES PLUS CHILLING TIME

¼ cup butter or soft margarine
¾ pound fresh mushrooms, sliced
1 small onion, minced
1 clove garlic, minced
1 cup pecans
½ teaspoon dried thyme
Dash nutmeg
Salt and freshly ground black pepper to taste
50 red cherry tomatoes, with insides scooped out

In a medium-size skillet, melt the butter and sauté the mushrooms, onion, and garlic until soft. Combine all the ingredients, except the tomatoes, in a blender or food processor and blend until smooth. Chill thoroughly.

Just before serving, stuff the tomatoes with the pâté. Serve the remaining pâté with crackers or bread.

Tofu Spread

YIELD: 8-10 SERVINGS
TIME: 20 MINUTES

●

½ pound tofu, cut into chunks
2 scallions, diced
¼ cup tahini (sesame seed paste)
2 tablespoons tamari or soy sauce
2 tablespoons fresh parsley
50 red cherry tomatoes, with insides scooped out

In a blender or food processor, blend all the ingredients until smooth. Stuff the mixture into the tomatoes. Serve the remaining spread on crackers or celery sticks.

Rosy Snow-Capped Tomatoes

YIELD: 6 SERVINGS
TIME: 30 MINUTES PLUS CHILLING TIME

12 firm, small to medium red tomatoes
1 carrot, grated
1 medium red bell pepper, cored, seeded, and finely diced
1 small onion, minced
1 small cucumber, peeled and grated
1 cup low-fat cottage cheese
4 ounces low-fat cream cheese
1½ cups *Rosy Cream Dressing* (see page 91)
Salt and freshly ground black pepper to taste
1 cup whipped topping

Hollow out the tomatoes and save the insides for the *Rosy Cream Dressing*. Turn the tomatoes upside down on paper towels to drain.

In a large bowl, mix the remaining vegetables with the cottage cheese, cream cheese, ½ cup *Rosy Cream Dressing*, salt, and pepper. Stuff the mixture into the tomatoes and set the tomatoes in a shallow casserole pan.

Fold the remaining *Rosy Cream Dressing* into the whipped topping. Pour this dressing over the tomatoes, cover lightly, and place in the freezer for 2 hours, or until the dressing begins to freeze slightly. Serve immediately.

Chicken Coronation in Tomatoes

YIELD: 6-8 SERVINGS
TIME: 35 MINUTES

2 tablespoons vegetable oil
1 medium onion, diced
1 large green bell pepper, cored, seeded, and diced
1 heaping teaspoon curry powder
¾ cup red wine
½ cup water
½ cup catsup
1 tablespoon apricot jam
6 cups cooked diced chicken
½ cup low-calorie mayonnaise
¾ cup whipped topping
Salt and freshly ground black pepper to taste
Fresh lemon juice to taste
8 firm, medium red tomatoes, with insides scooped out

In a large skillet, heat the oil and sauté the onion and green pepper for 5 minutes. Add the curry powder and cook for 5 minutes. Add the wine, water, catsup, and apricot jam. Simmer gently for 10 minutes, or until the sauce is slightly reduced. Set aside to cool.

Mix the cooled sauce with the chicken. Fold in the mayonnaise and whipped topping. Add the salt, pepper, and lemon juice. Fill the tomatoes with the chicken mixture and serve.

Spinach Stuffed Tomatoes

YIELD: 4-6 SERVINGS
TIME: 40 MINUTES

2 tablespoons butter or soft margarine
2 cloves garlic, minced
2 tablespoons unbleached all-purpose flour
¾ cup low-fat milk
2 cups cooked chopped spinach
½ teaspoon dried thyme
2 teaspoons fresh lemon juice
Salt and freshly ground black pepper to taste
6 firm, medium red tomatoes, with insides scooped out

Preheat oven to 350° F. In a medium-size saucepan, melt the butter and sauté the garlic for 5 minutes. Do not brown. Stir in the flour. Slowly add the milk, stirring constantly to prevent lumps. Add the remaining ingredients.

Pour the filling into the tomatoes and place the tomatoes in a baking dish. Bake for 20 minutes and serve.

Italian Spinach Tomatoes

YIELD: 4-6 SERVINGS
TIME: 25 MINUTES

2 cups cooked chopped spinach
½ teaspoon garlic powder
1 teaspoon dried thyme
1 teaspoon dried basil
1 egg
Salt and freshly ground black pepper to taste
1½ cups grated Parmesan cheese
6 firm, medium red tomatoes, with insides scooped out

Preheat oven to 350° F. In a large bowl, combine all the ingredients, except ¼ cup Parmesan cheese and the tomatoes.

Divide the spinach mixture among the tomatoes. Sprinkle the top of each tomato with the remaining cheese. Bake for 15 minutes and serve.

Stuffed Spanish Tomatoes

YIELD: 6-8 SERVINGS
TIME: 1 HOUR 10 MINUTES

8 firm, large red tomatoes
1 pound lean bulk sausage
2 tablespoons vegetable oil
1 large onion, diced
½ pound fresh mushrooms, sliced
1½ cups finely diced ham
1 cup bread crumbs
1 cup grated Parmesan cheese
Salt and freshly ground black pepper to taste
2 cloves garlic, minced
2 teaspoons dried basil
2 tablespoons unbleached all-purpose flour

Preheat oven to 350° F. Hollow out the inside of the tomatoes and reserve the pulp for the sauce. Turn the tomatoes upside down on paper towels to drain.

In a large skillet, brown the sausage, remove from skillet, and set aside. Drain off the fat. In the same skillet, heat the oil and sauté half the onion and all of the mushrooms until the onion is translucent and the mushrooms are soft. Combine the onion mixture with the sausage. Add the ham, half the bread crumbs, and half the cheese. Add the salt and pepper.

Divide the stuffing among the tomatoes. Sprinkle the remaining bread crumbs and cheese on top.

SAUCE: Combine the reserved tomato pulp, the remaining onion, garlic, and basil in a small saucepan. Simmer for 15 minutes. Pour this mixture in a blender or food processor, add the flour, and blend until smooth. Add salt and pepper to taste. Pour the sauce over the tomatoes and bake for 30 minutes, or until the sauce is bubbly.

Greek Stuffed Tomatoes

YIELD: 4-6 SERVINGS
TIME: 30 MINUTES

2 tablespoons olive oil
1 small onion, diced
2 cups cooked chopped spinach
2 teaspoons dried basil
½ cup bread crumbs
1 egg
½ pound feta cheese, crumbled
Salt and freshly ground black pepper to taste
6 firm, medium red tomatoes, with insides scooped out

Preheat oven to 350° F. In a small saucepan, heat the oil and sauté the onion for 10 minutes or until translucent. Combine all the remaining ingredients, except the tomatoes, and add to the onion.

Stuff the filling into the tomatoes. Bake for 15 minutes and serve.

Best Brunch Eggs

YIELD: 4-6 SERVINGS
TIME: 1 HOUR

½ cup butter or soft margarine
½ cup unbleached all-purpose flour
2 cups low-fat milk
1 pound low-fat cheddar cheese, grated
1 tablespoon Dijon mustard
Dash Worcestershire sauce
Salt and freshly ground black pepper to taste
6 firm, large red tomatoes, with insides scooped out
Salt and freshly ground black pepper to taste
1 cup grated low-fat cheddar cheese
6 eggs

Melt the butter in a large saucepan on medium heat. Stir in the flour. Slowly add the milk, a little at a time, stirring constantly to prevent lumps. Add 1 pound cheese, mustard, Worcestershire sauce, salt, and pepper. Continue cooking until the sauce is thick and smooth, stirring constantly. Set aside.

Preheat oven to 350° F. Oil a baking dish and arrange the tomatoes in the dish. Sprinkle the insides of the tomatoes with the salt, pepper, and 1 cup cheese. Break the eggs into the tomatoes and spoon the cheese sauce on top. Bake for 20-30 minutes, or until the eggs are set.

2

Red Tomato Specialties

Tomato Juice Drinks

Tomato juice is very adaptable. Here are some recipes for vegetable and herb combinations. Each drink is made with *1 cup of tomato juice* combined with the other ingredients in a blender and served over ice. Use vegetable sticks — strips of green bell peppers, stalks of celery, carrot sticks, or scallions — as stirrers and garnishes.

NEW ORLEANS SIPPER: Combine 1 strip green bell pepper, 1 teaspoon fresh lemon juice, dash Worcestershire sauce, dash cayenne powder, dash garlic powder, and 1 thick slice avocado.

SOUTH OF THE BORDER: Combine ½ teaspoon ground cumin, 2 teaspoons *Red Taco Sauce*, (see page 118), dash cayenne powder.

SUMMER COOLER: Combine 1 stalk celery diced, ½ teaspoon fresh mint, and crushed ice.

FRENCH CONNECTION: Combine ½ cup peeled cucumber diced and ½ teaspoon dried tarragon.

DILLY CUKES: Combine ½ cup peeled cucumber diced, 1 large scallion minced, ½ teaspoon dried dill, and crushed ice.

HERE'S TO YOUR HEALTH: Combine 1 stalk celery diced, 3 heaping tablespoons plain, low-fat yogurt, 1 teaspoon fresh lemon juice, dash Worcestershire sauce, and dash Tabasco sauce.

SOME LIKE IT HOT: Mix 1 tablespoon prepared horseradish with 1 teaspoon fresh lemon juice.

SUGAR & SPICE: Combine ½ teaspoon ground cinnamon, pinch ground fennel, and 1 teaspoon honey.

ORIENT EXPRESS: Combine 1 teaspoon tamari, dash Five-Spice Powder, and 1 large scallion minced.

THE MEDITERRANEAN: Combine ½ teaspoon dried basil, dash dried thyme, dash garlic powder, and 1 teaspoon fresh lemon juice.

BUNNY'S FAVORITE: Combine 1 small carrot diced, 2 sprigs fresh parsley, 1 strip green bell pepper, dash freshly ground black pepper, and dash Tabasco sauce.

THE TEXAN'S HAT: Combine ½ cup beef broth and dash spicy steak sauce.

ANGLER'S NET: Combine ¼ cup clam juice and ½ stalk celery diced.

RUSSIAN COCKTAIL: Combine ½ teaspoon caraway seeds and dash ground fennel. Top with plain, low-fat yogurt.

Rosy Cheese Wafers

YIELD: 60 WAFERS
TIME: 45 MINUTES PLUS CHILLING TIME

¼ pound butter or soft margarine, at room temperature
½ pound Brie or low-fat cheddar cheese, cubed
1⅓ cups unbleached all-purpose flour
½ teaspoon Tabasco sauce
¼ teaspoon salt
¼ cup tomato paste
¼ cup poppy, caraway, or sesame seeds

In a food processor fitted with a metal blade or with an electric mixer, cream together the butter and cheese. Add the flour, Tabasco sauce, salt, and tomato paste. Mix together until a ball is formed. Divide the dough into four parts and form into logs, 1 inch in diameter. Wrap in wax paper and chill until firm.

Preheat oven to 400° F. Slice the logs into ¼-inch circles and arrange 1 inch apart on an ungreased baking sheet. Sprinkle the poppy seeds on each wafer. Bake for 8-10 minutes, or until the edges are golden. Serve immediately.

Super-Duper Nachos

YIELD: 6 SERVINGS
TIME: 20 MINUTES

12 cooked corn tortillas
¾ cup *Red Taco Sauce* (see page 118)
1 medium ripe avocado, peeled and diced
1 cup grated low-fat cheddar or Monterey Jack cheese

Preheat oven to 400° F. Cut the tortillas into triangles and arrange in a shallow baking dish. Spread the *Red Taco Sauce* over the tortillas, leaving a corner of each tortilla uncovered to make them easier to pick up. Sprinkle the avocado pieces and the grated cheese on top. Bake for 10 minutes.

Broil for 5 minutes, or until the cheese is bubbly brown. Serve hot.

VARIATION: Sprinkle cooked lean ground beef on top before the nachos are baked.

Caponatina

YIELD: 4-5 CUPS
TIME: 55 MINUTES

2 tablespoons butter or soft margarine
2 tablespoons olive oil
1 medium eggplant, unpeeled and cut into ¼-inch slices
1 cup chopped onions
1 cup thinly sliced celery
1 cup chopped red or green bell peppers
3 cloves garlic, minced
2 medium red tomatoes, chopped
2 tablespoons chopped fresh parsley
2 teaspoons chopped fresh basil *or* ½ teaspoon dried basil
1 tablespoon chopped fresh oregano *or* 1 teaspoon dried oregano
2 tablespoons fresh lemon juice
1 tablespoon red wine vinegar
Freshly ground black pepper to taste
½ cup green olives
½ cup toasted pine nuts*
Lemon wedges
Toasted pita bread wedges

In a large skillet, melt the butter with the oil. Cook the eggplant slices, several at a time, until golden brown. Remove and drain on paper towels.

In the same skillet, combine the onions, celery, bell peppers, and garlic. Add the tomatoes, parsley, basil, and oregano. Cook until slightly thick. Remove from heat.

Chop the eggplant slices and combine with the tomato mixture. Mix well. Stir in the lemon juice, vinegar, and black pepper. Mix in the olives. Refrigerate, covered, until the flavors blend. To serve, sprinkle with the pine nuts and garnish with the lemon and bread wedges.

**To toast the pine nuts*, place in a small skillet on low heat. Cook until lightly browned, stirring constantly.

. . . .

Barbecued Wings

YIELD: 4 SERVINGS
TIME: 1 HOUR

12 chicken wings
1 cup tomato sauce
3 tablespoons brown sugar
1 tablespoon tamari or soy sauce

Preheat oven to 400° F. In a shallow baking pan, arrange the chicken wings so they do not touch each other. Bake for 30 minutes.

In a medium-size saucepan, combine the tomato sauce, brown sugar, and tamari and cook until the brown sugar has dissolved.

After the chicken wings are cooked, thickly spread the sauce over the wings and bake for 30-40 minutes more or until browned and very tender. Serve warm.

Salsa con Queso

YIELD: 8 SERVINGS
TIME: 15 MINUTES

2 tablespoons vegetable oil
1 medium onion, diced
2 medium red tomatoes, finely diced
8 ounces low-fat cream cheese
½ pound Monterey Jack cheese, grated
1 jalapeño pepper, seeded and finely diced
2 teaspoons chile powder
Corn chips

In a medium-size skillet, heat the oil and sauté the onion for 5 minutes. Add the tomatoes and simmer for 5 minutes more.

Reduce heat and add the remaining ingredients, except the corn chips. Cook, stirring constantly, until the cheeses are melted. Serve warm with the corn chips.

Salsa

YIELD: 1½ CUPS
TIME: 10 MINUTES

2 medium red tomatoes, finely chopped
½ cup finely chopped green bell pepper
1 sereno chile pepper, seeded and very finely diced
1 small onion, finely diced
2 cloves garlic, minced
Juice of 1 lemon
Salt and freshly ground black pepper to taste

In a medium-size bowl, mix all the ingredients and serve with corn chips or as a taco sauce.

Hélène's Salsa

YIELD: 3½ CUPS
TIME: 10 MINUTES

One 28-ounce can whole tomatoes, with liquid
One 8-ounce can tomato sauce
2-3 jalapeño peppers, seeded and finely chopped (optional)
1-2 canned green chiles, chopped
½ cup diced onions
½ teaspoon sugar
2 teaspoons white vinegar
1 teaspoon ground cumin
Dash dried oregano
Salt and freshly ground black pepper to taste
Low-fat cream cheese
Corn chips

In a large bowl, mash the tomatoes with a fork. In a medium-size bowl, combine the remaining ingredients, except the cream cheese and corn chips. Add the tomatoes and mix well. Serve over the cream cheese with the corn chips on the side.

Salsa de Tomatillo

YIELD: 1½ CUPS
TIME: 10 MINUTES

Raw tomatoes can be used for this sauce. Some cooks, however, prefer to cook them first, by simmering gently in water to cover for 20 minutes, stirring occasionally.

½ pound tomatillos, husked, rinsed, and cut in half
2 serrano chile peppers, fresh or canned
or 2 canned green chiles, plus hot sauce to taste
½ teaspoon minced garlic
3 tablespoons minced onions
¼ cup chopped fresh cilantro
Dash salt
Dash sugar

In a blender or food processor, chop all the ingredients, adding a little water, if needed. For a typical Mexican *salsa*, stop processing when the mixture is still chunky. Serve.

The TOMATILLO, a gift from Mexico, has a husk-like outer skin and does not look particularly edible. It happens to be delicious and those who like Mexican cooking have been buying tomatillos in cans for years. As with most things, fresh is better, and they are now available in many produce departments — or you can grow your own. Tomatillos taste a bit like regular green tomatoes, but they have a character all their own.

To use, remove the papery husk, then wash and dry. The tomatillos are now ready to be cooked, whole or chopped, in any type of soup or stew. Tomatillos also can be grown from seed. Be careful, there are similar sounding vegetables in many seed catalogs. What you want is *physalis ixocarpa.*

Guacamole

YIELD: 1½ CUPS
TIME: 15 MINUTES

If not served within an hour, Guacamole *will begin to darken. Placing plastic wrap directly on top of the* Guacamole *will slow the darkening process. For a slightly different taste, lemons may be substituted for limes.*

2 medium ripe avocados, peeled
¼ cup diced red tomatoes
Juice of 2 limes
1 tablespoon minced onions
¼ teaspoon Tabasco sauce
1 tablespoon chopped fresh cilantro *or* 1 teaspoon dried coriander
¼ teaspoon ground cumin
Freshly ground black pepper to taste

Cut the avocados in half and remove pits. In a serving bowl, mash the avocados with the back of a fork. Add the remaining ingredients and mix well. The *Guacamole* should be chunky. Serve as a dip with corn chips or as a topping for Mexican dishes.

Guacamole with Sour Cream

YIELD: 4 SERVINGS
TIME: 15 MINUTES

2 large ripe avocados, peeled
2 large red tomatoes, chopped
2 tablespoons chopped onions
1 tablespoon chopped fresh cilantro
1 tablespoon fresh lemon juice
1 clove garlic, minced
1 small red chile pepper, seeded and finely chopped
or hot pepper sauce to taste
1 teaspoon ground paprika
Salt and freshly ground black pepper to taste
4 tablespoons low-fat sour cream
Corn chips (optional)
Vegetable sticks (optional)

Cut the avocados in half and remove the pits. In a serving bowl, mash the avocados with the back of a fork. Add the remaining ingredients, except the sour cream, and mix well. The *Guacamole* should be chunky.

Top with the sour cream and serve immediately with the corn chips or vegetable sticks.

Tomato Swiss Cheese Soup

YIELD: 12 SERVINGS
TIME: 1 HOUR

½ cup butter or soft margarine
¾ cup unbleached all-purpose flour
4 cups low-fat milk
4 cups tomato juice or puree
¾ pound Swiss cheese, grated
2 teaspoons dried thyme
1 teaspoon dried basil
Salt and freshly ground black pepper to taste
Herb croutons, for garnish

In a large pot, melt the butter. Add the flour and stir, mashing any lumps with the back of a spoon. Cook for 2 minutes.

Slowly add the milk a little at a time, stirring after each addition until smooth. Add the remaining ingredients, except the croutons, and reduce heat. Cook until the cheese is melted. Do *not* boil this soup, as it will curdle and the cheese will form into tiny lumps. Garnish with the croutons and serve.

Cream of Tomato Soup with Wine

YIELD: 12 SERVINGS
TIME: 1 HOUR

4 tablespoons butter or soft margarine
1 large onion, diced
3 cloves garlic, minced
10 large red tomatoes, chopped
½ cup unbleached all-purpose flour
2 cups chicken or vegetable broth
1 pint half-and-half
1 cup dry white wine
Salt and freshly ground black pepper to taste
Fresh lemon juice to taste
1 sprig fresh dill *or* 1 tablespoon dried dill for each bowl

In a large pot, melt the butter and sauté the onion and garlic until translucent. Add the tomatoes. Cook over medium heat for 5 minutes. Sprinkle the flour over the tomatoes and stir well. Add the remaining ingredients, except the lemon juice and dill, and cook for 30 minutes.

In a blender or food processor, puree the soup until smooth. Reheat gently and add the salt and pepper. Add the lemon juice and garnish with the dill. Serve immediately.

Cream of Tomato Soup

YIELD: 4-6 SERVINGS
TIME: 40 MINUTES

4 cups chopped red tomatoes
1 medium onion, chopped
4 whole cloves
6 black peppercorns
1 teaspoon brown sugar
1 teaspoon salt
½ cup chopped fresh parsley
3 tablespoons butter or soft margarine
3 tablespoons unbleached all-purpose flour
1½ cups chicken broth
1 cup half-and-half

In a large saucepan, combine the tomatoes, onion, cloves, peppercorns, brown sugar, salt, and parsley. Simmer for 10 minutes. In a blender or food processor, blend the tomato mixture for 15 seconds. Set aside.

In the same saucepan, melt the butter and add the flour, stirring until golden. Add the chicken broth and stir until thick. Add the reserved tomato mixture and half-and-half. Heat thoroughly and serve.

Tomato & Onion Soup

YIELD: 4 SERVINGS
TIME: 50 MINUTES

3 tablespoons butter or soft margarine
2 tablespoons vegetable oil
3 large onions, thinly sliced
2 cups tomato sauce
4 cups chicken broth or water
1 teaspoon sugar
½ teaspoon ground nutmeg
Salt to taste
8 thin slices warm French bread
½ cup grated Gruyère cheese

In a large saucepan, melt the butter with the oil. Add the onions and stir well. Cover the saucepan and cook on very low heat for 30-40 minutes, or until the onions are very soft. Add the tomato sauce, chicken broth, sugar, nutmeg, and salt. Bring to a boil.

Place two slices bread in each bowl and sprinkle with half of the cheese. Pour the soup over the bread and sprinkle with the remaining cheese. Serve immediately.

Tomato Clam Broth

YIELD: 4 SERVINGS
TIME: 50 MINUTES

●

2 tablespoons butter or soft margarine
1 medium carrot, chopped
1 stalk celery, chopped
1 small green bell pepper, cored, seeded, and diced
1 small onion, chopped
2 cups tomato sauce
2 cups clam broth
1 cup white wine
Salt and freshly ground black pepper to taste
Fresh parsley, for garnish

In a large saucepan, melt the butter and sauté the carrot, celery, green pepper, and onion until soft. Add the tomato sauce and clam broth. Bring to a boil. Reduce heat and simmer, covered, for 30 minutes. Strain.

In the same saucepan, return the tomato and clam broth and combine with the wine, salt, and pepper. Simmer for 10 minutes. Garnish with the parsley and serve immediately.

Tortilla Soup

YIELD: 6-8 SERVINGS
TIME: 1 HOUR

2 tablespoons vegetable oil
1 large onion, diced
5 stalks celery, diced
One 28-ounce can whole tomatoes, with liquid
2 cups water or chicken broth
Salt and freshly ground black pepper to taste
Dash Tabasco sauce
12 soft corn tortillas
½ pound Monterey Jack cheese, grated
2 medium ripe avocados, peeled and diced
1 cup low-fat sour cream

Preheat oven to 350° F. In a large pot, heat the oil and sauté the onion and celery. Just as the onion becomes limp and translucent, add the tomatoes, water, salt, pepper, and Tabasco sauce. Break the tomatoes up with a spoon. Cover the pot and simmer gently for 45 minutes.

Stack the tortillas in two piles and cut them into long strips. Spread the strips on a baking sheet and bake for 20 minutes or until crispy.

Before serving, put some of the cheese and avocado into each soup bowl. Stand the tortilla strips around the inside edge of each bowl so that they stand above the rims of the bowls. Ladle the hot soup over the cheese and avocado and garnish with a dollop of the sour cream. Serve immediately.

Hungarian Cabbage & Tomato Soup

YIELD: 10 SERVINGS
TIME: 1 HOUR

3 tablespoons vegetable oil
1 large onion, diced
8 cups shredded green cabbage
½ cup unbleached all-purpose flour
4 cups *Stewed Tomatoes* (see page 94) *or* 4 cups chopped red tomatoes
2 cups tomato juice or puree
1 tablespoon caraway seeds
2 cups chicken broth or water
2 tablespoons honey or sugar
Juice of 1 lemon
Salt and freshly ground black pepper to taste
1 cup low-fat sour cream (optional)

In a large pot, heat the oil. Add the onion and cabbage and cook until the cabbage is limp but not browned. Sprinkle the flour over the cabbage and mix well.

Add the remaining ingredients, except the sour cream, and cover the pot. Simmer for at least 30 minutes, or as long as possible. Serve with the sour cream as a garnish.

VARIATIONS: This soup is equally delicious when made without oil, if the cabbage and onion are cooked in a little water first to wilt them.

Add 1 cup diced beets with the tomatoes and the color of the soup changes from red to deep purple — a wonderful borscht.

Rosy Potato Leek Soup

YIELD: 8 SERVINGS
TIME: 1 HOUR

2 tablespoons vegetable oil
4 medium leeks, sliced (white part only)
4 medium potatoes, diced
4 medium red tomatoes, chopped
5 cups chicken or vegetable broth
2 teaspoons dried dill
1 cup half-and-half
Salt and freshly ground black pepper to taste
Dried dill, for garnish

In a large pot, heat the oil and sauté the leeks on medium heat for 10 minutes. Add the potatoes, tomatoes, chicken broth, and dill. Cover the pot and simmer for 30 minutes. Cool slightly.

In a blender or food processor, puree the soup in small amounts until smooth. Reheat gently and add the half-and-half. Add the salt and pepper. Serve hot or cold, garnished with the additional dill.

Eight Bean Soup

YIELD: 8 SERVINGS
TIME: 3 HOURS 30 MINUTES PLUS SOAKING TIME

¼ cup *each* red kidney beans, green split peas, yellow split peas, lentils, black-eyed peas, navy beans, lima beans, and pinto beans
2 tablespoons barley
2 quarts water
1 ham bone
1 bay leaf
2 cloves garlic, crushed
1 cup chopped onions
One 28-ounce can crushed tomatoes
1 tablespoon chile powder
2 tablespoons fresh lemon juice
½ teaspoon dried thyme
1 teaspoon dried savory

Wash the beans and barley thoroughly. Place the beans and barley in a large pot. Cover with water and soak overnight. Drain and discard the water.

Return the beans and barley to the pot and add the water, ham bone, bay leaf, and garlic. Simmer gently for 2½-3 hours.

Add the remaining ingredients and simmer for 30 minutes more. Remove the ham bone and bay leaf and serve.

Sausage & Vegetable Soup with Lentils

YIELD: 4-6 SERVINGS
TIME: 1 HOUR

4 tablespoons vegetable oil
1 pound lean pork sausage links
1 cup chopped celery
1 cup chopped onions
1 clove garlic, minced
1 cup thinly sliced carrots
2 cups canned crushed tomatoes
4 cups chicken or beef broth
½ teaspoon dried thyme
½ teaspoon dried marjoram
½ teaspoon dried parsley
1 cup lentils

In a large pot, heat 2 tablespoons oil and sauté the sausages until evenly browned. Drain off the fat. Remove the sausages with a slotted spoon and keep warm.

In the same pot, heat the remaining oil and add the celery, onions, garlic, and carrots and sauté for 10 minutes, or until the onions are translucent. Add the tomatoes, chicken broth, and herbs.

Cut the reserved sausages into 1-inch slices and return to the pot. Bring the soup to a boil. Add the lentils and reduce heat. Simmer, uncovered, for 30 minutes, or until the lentils are tender and the sausages are thoroughly cooked. Serve immediately.

Turkey Minestrone

YIELD: 12 SERVINGS
TIME: 45 MINUTES

8 cups turkey broth
2 cups cooked chopped turkey
1 medium onion, chopped
1 stalk celery, chopped
1 cup chopped red tomatoes
1 cup chopped zucchini
1 cup cooked white beans
1 teaspoon salt
1 teaspoon chopped fresh thyme *or* ½ teaspoon dried thyme
1 tablespoon chopped fresh parsley *or* 1½ teaspoons dried parsley
2 cups uncooked noodles

In a very large pot, bring the broth to a boil. Add the turkey, onion, celery, and tomatoes. Simmer for 20 minutes. Add the zucchini, beans, salt, thyme, parsley, and noodles. Continue to simmer until the noodles are very soft and all the flavors have blended. Serve hot.

Slumgullion

YIELD: 4-6 SERVINGS
TIME: 45 MINUTES

8 ounces macaroni pasta
1½ cups green beans, topped and tailed
1½ cups sliced carrots
1 pound lean ground beef
½ cup diced onions
¼ cup minced fresh parsley
Dash garlic powder
½ teaspoon dried oregano
⅛ teaspoon dried marjoram
1 teaspoon caraway seeds
Dash dried sage
4 cups chopped red tomatoes
Salt and freshly ground black pepper to taste
½ cup grated low-fat sharp cheddar cheese

Cook the macaroni according to package directions. Drain and set aside. In a small saucepan, cook the green beans and carrots in as little water as possible until tender crisp. Set aside.

In a large skillet, sauté the ground beef and onions until the meat is browned and the onions are soft. Drain off the fat. Stir in the parsley, garlic powder, oregano, marjoram, caraway seeds, and sage. Mix well.

Add the tomatoes, reserved macaroni, reserved green beans and carrots, salt, and pepper. Simmer for 20-30 minutes. Before serving, stir in the cheese. Serve immediately.

Tomato Corn Chowder

YIELD: 10 SERVINGS
TIME: 30 MINUTES

½ cup butter or soft margarine
½ cup unbleached all-purpose flour
4 cups low-fat milk
8 cups *Stewed Tomatoes* (see page 94) *or* 8 cups canned tomatoes
4 cups whole kernel corn, fresh or frozen
Salt and freshly ground black pepper to taste
Herb croutons, for garnish
Minced black olives, for garnish

In a large pot, melt the butter over medium heat. Mix in the flour to make a smooth paste. Slowly add the milk a little at a time and continue stirring to prevent lumps.

Add the *Stewed Tomatoes* and corn. Cook on low heat until the corn is heated through. Add the salt and pepper. Serve hot and garnish each bowl with the croutons or the black olives.

Italian Fish Chowder

YIELD: 4-6 SERVINGS
TIME: 45 MINUTES

2 tablespoons olive oil
1 medium onion, diced
1 medium zucchini, diced
1 large green bell pepper, cored, seeded, and diced
2 cloves garlic, minced
4 cups tomato juice or puree
¼ cup chopped fresh parsley
1 teaspoon dried basil
½ teaspoon dried oregano
1 teaspoon dried thyme
½ cup red or white wine
1 cup cooked white rice *or* ¼ cup uncooked white rice
2 cups water
½ pound boneless fish, cut into pieces *or* 1 cup minced clams
or ½ pound medium shrimp, peeled and deveined
Salt and freshly ground black pepper to taste
Grated Parmesan cheese, for garnish

In a large pot, heat the oil and sauté the onion, zucchini, green pepper, and garlic for 10 minutes. Add the tomato juice, herbs, wine, rice, and water. Simmer for 15-20 minutes.

Add the fish and cook for at least 10 minutes on low heat. This soup improves in flavor the longer it is cooked. Add the salt and pepper and serve garnished with the Parmesan cheese.

VARIATION: Small meatballs made from lean bulk sausage can be simmered in water until cooked, and added to the soup, instead of the fish.

Cioppino

YIELD: 6 SERVINGS
TIME: 45 MINUTES

●

½ cup vegetable oil
½ cup chopped onions
½ cup chopped scallions (include green tops)
1 medium green bell pepper, cored, seeded, and chopped
2 cloves garlic, minced
3 cups tomato sauce
2 cups red wine
1 bay leaf
Salt and freshly ground black pepper to taste
2 pounds firm white fish, cut into large pieces
1 cooked lobster or Dungeness crab, cut into pieces
1 pound medium shrimp, peeled and deveined
1 pint clams or mussels, shucked

In a large pot, heat the oil. Add the onions, scallions, green pepper, and garlic and cook until soft. Add the tomato sauce, wine, bay leaf, salt, and pepper. Bring to a boil and simmer for 10 minutes.

Add the fish, lobster, and shrimp and cook for 15 minutes. Add the clams and cook for 5 minutes more. Serve very hot.

Tomato Tuna Gumbo

YIELD: 8 SERVINGS
TIME: 1 HOUR

3 tablespoons olive oil
2 medium onions, diced
3 cloves garlic, minced
1 large eggplant, unpeeled and diced
4 cups diced okra, fresh or frozen
2 medium green bell peppers, cored, seeded, and diced
12 medium red tomatoes, chopped
½ cup tomato paste
1 cup chicken broth or water
¼ cup minced fresh parsley
1 bay leaf
1 teaspoon dried thyme
1 teaspoon dried basil
1½ teaspoons Worcestershire sauce
Dash cayenne powder
Salt and freshly ground black pepper to taste
One 12-ounce can water-packed solid white tuna, drained
3 cups cooked white rice

In a large pot, heat the oil and sauté the onions and garlic. Add the remaining vegetables and cook for 15 minutes. Add the tomato paste, chicken broth, herbs, Worcestershire sauce, cayenne powder, salt, pepper, and tuna. Cover and cook for 20 minutes more. Remove the bay leaf. Serve over the cooked rice.

Chicken Gumbo

YIELD: 6 SERVINGS
TIME: 40 MINUTES

2 slices lean bacon, diced
1 tablespoon vegetable oil
1 large onion, chopped
1 small green bell pepper, cored, seeded, and chopped
1½ cups thickly sliced okra, fresh or frozen
1 stalk celery, chopped
2 cups cooked red tomatoes
1½ cups chicken broth
1½ cups cooked chopped chicken
1 bay leaf
¼ teaspoon hot pepper sauce
½ teaspoon chopped fresh thyme *or* ¼ teaspoon dried thyme
Salt to taste
Cooked rice

In a small skillet, cook the bacon until crisp. Drain off the fat and set the bacon aside.

In a large pot, heat the oil on very high heat and sauté the onion, green pepper, okra, and celery until soft, stirring constantly. (Quick high heat seals the okra to prevent long, gelatinous, okra strings in the gumbo.)

Add the reserved bacon, tomatoes, chicken broth, chicken, bay leaf, hot pepper sauce, thyme, and salt to the pot. Bring to a boil and simmer gently for 20-30 minutes, or until the okra is just tender. Do not overcook. Remove the bay leaf. Serve over the rice.

Chicken & Barley Stew

YIELD: 6 SERVINGS
TIME: 2 HOURS

2 tablespoons vegetable oil
6 chicken legs or thighs, with skin removed
2 medium onions, chopped
1 stalk celery, chopped
1 medium carrot, chopped
1 small slice ham, chopped *or* 1 cup leftover ham pieces
1 cup dry white wine
1½ cups chopped red tomatoes, fresh or canned
1 clove garlic, minced
3 tablespoons chopped fresh parsley *or* 1 tablespoon dried parsley
1 teaspoon chopped fresh thyme *or* ½ teaspoon dried thyme
½ cup uncooked barley
Salt to taste

In a large pot, heat the oil and sauté the chicken slowly until cooked. Stir in the onions, celery, and carrot and cook until the vegetables are slightly softened.

Add the ham, wine, tomatoes, and garlic. Bring to a boil and stir in the parsley and thyme. Reduce heat, cover, and simmer gently for 30 minutes. Add the barley and cook for 1 hour more. Add the salt and serve.

Argentine Puchero

YIELD: 6-8 SERVINGS
TIME: 1 HOUR 30 MINUTES

¼ cup olive oil
One 3½-4-pound chicken, cut-up and skin removed
1 pound lean, boneless lamb, cut into 2-inch cubes
4 medium onions, thinly sliced
5 cloves garlic, minced
1 large carrot, chopped
2 medium zucchini, cut into ½-inch slices
or one 3-pound pumpkin, peeled and cut into ½-inch cubes
1 tablespoon dried thyme
⅛ teaspoon cayenne powder
1 cup red wine
2 cups chicken broth
4 cups chopped red tomatoes with juice
3 cups whole kernel corn, fresh or frozen
3 tablespoons cornstarch
2 tablespoons water

In a large pot, heat 2 tablespoons oil and sauté the chicken for 2 minutes on each side. Remove the chicken and set aside.

Add the lamb to the pot and brown for 2 minutes. Remove the lamb and set aside. Drain off the fat.

In the same pot, heat the remaining oil and sauté the onions, garlic, and carrot for 5 minutes. Add the zucchini and cook for 3 minutes. Add the thyme and cayenne powder, wine, chicken broth, and tomatoes. Mix well. Add the reserved chicken and lamb and simmer gently for 40 minutes. Add the corn and cook for 10 minutes.

In a small bowl, combine the cornstarch and water to make a smooth paste. Stir the paste into the pot to thicken. Serve.

. . . .

Eggplant Stew

YIELD: 4 SERVINGS
TIME: 1 HOUR

●

Plum tomatoes are suggested for this recipe because they have thick pulp and little juice.

1 small eggplant, unpeeled and cut into ¼-inch cubes
¼ cup vegetable oil
2 tablespoons chopped onions
1 clove garlic, minced
3 fresh basil leaves
2 tablespoons chopped fresh parsley
4 plum tomatoes, peeled and sliced
1 teaspoon salt
⅛ teaspoon freshly ground black pepper
¼ teaspoon dried oregano
1 teaspoon sugar

In a large pot, combine the eggplant with the oil, onions, garlic, basil, and parsley. Mix well to completely coat the eggplant lightly with oil. Cook on high heat for 7 minutes, stirring frequently.

Add the tomatoes, salt, pepper, oregano, and sugar. Cover the pot and simmer for 15-20 minutes, or until the eggplant is tender, stirring frequently. Serve very hot.

Hungarian Goulash

YIELD: 6 SERVINGS
TIME: 2 HOURS 25 MINUTES

2 pounds lean beef chuck, cut into ½-inch cubes
1 cup unbleached all-purpose flour
3 tablespoons vegetable oil
2 large onions, chopped
1 clove garlic, minced
1 cup tomato sauce
1 cup red wine
1 bay leaf
1 teaspoon dried thyme
¼ cup chopped fresh parsley
Salt and freshly ground black pepper to taste
1 tablespoon ground Hungarian paprika

Dredge the beef in the flour. In a large skillet, heat the oil and brown the meat on all sides. Remove the beef and set aside.

In the same skillet, sauté the onions and garlic. Stir in the tomato sauce, wine, bay leaf, thyme, parsley, salt, and pepper. Bring to a boil.

Reduce heat and add the reserved meat. Cover and simmer for 2 hours, or until the meat is very tender. Stir in the paprika and simmer for 15 minutes more. Remove the bay leaf. Serve.

Albóndigas

YIELD: 6-8 SERVINGS
TIME: 1 HOUR 15 MINUTES

8 cups beef broth
2 medium green bell peppers, cored, seeded, and cut into strips
2 medium red bell peppers, cored, seeded, and cut into strips
2 medium onions, chopped
2 medium carrots, diced
½ cup diced turnips
One 28-ounce can plum tomatoes
2 pounds lean ground beef
Salt and freshly ground black pepper to taste
1 clove garlic, minced
⅛ teaspoon Tabasco sauce
1 teaspoon Worcestershire sauce
1 teaspoon ground cumin
1 tablespoon vegetable oil

In a large pot, combine the beef broth, bell peppers, onions, carrots, and turnips. Bring to a boil. Reduce heat and simmer, covered, for 20-30 minutes, or until the vegetables are tender crisp. Add the tomatoes and cook 10 minutes more.

In a large bowl, combine the ground beef with the remaining ingredients, except the oil, and shape into small meatballs. In a medium-size skillet, heat the oil and quickly brown the meatballs. Drain off the fat. Add the meatballs to the pot and cook for 10 minutes. Serve.

VARIATION: Serve with small dishes of grated low-fat cheddar cheese, chopped fresh parsley, chopped onions, chopped water chestnuts, and herb croutons.

Knock-Your-Socks-Off Chile

YIELD: 6-8 SERVINGS
TIME: 2 HOURS 25 MINUTES

4 tablespoons vegetable oil
2 pounds lean ground beef
1 pound lean pork, cut into ½-inch cubes
4 cups coarsely chopped onions
3 cloves garlic, minced
1 cup chopped green bell peppers
3 tablespoons chile powder *or* to taste
½ cup beer
4 cups tomato sauce
¾ cup tomato paste
4 medium red tomatoes, coarsely chopped
1 teaspoon ground cumin
1 bay leaf
½ teaspoon freshly ground black pepper
1 teaspoon dried oregano
4 cups cooked red kidney beans
1 cup shredded low-fat cheddar cheese
3 soft flour tortillas, cut into wedges

In a large pot, heat 2 tablespoons oil and brown the beef and pork. Drain off the fat. In the same pot, heat the remaining oil and stir in the onions, garlic, and green pepper and cook until tender. Add the chile powder, beer, tomato sauce and paste, tomatoes, cumin, bay leaf, black pepper, and oregano. Mix well. Simmer slowly for 1 hour 30 minutes, stirring occasionally.

Add the beans and cook 30 minutes more. Remove the bay leaf. Serve sprinkled with the cheese and the tortilla wedges on the side.

Ground Turkey Chile

YIELD: 8 SERVINGS
TIME: 2 HOURS 45 MINUTES

●

1 tablespoon vegetable oil
1 large onion, chopped
1 small green bell pepper, cored, seeded, and chopped
1 pound lean ground turkey
1 cup tomato sauce
4 cups chopped red tomatoes
2 cups water
1 clove garlic, minced
2 tablespoons chile powder
1 teaspoon ground paprika
½ teaspoon dried oregano
½ teaspoon ground cumin
¼ teaspoon cayenne powder *or* to taste
2 cups cooked pinto beans
¼ cup fine cornmeal mixed in ¾ cup cold water

In a large pot, heat the oil and sauté the onion and green pepper until soft. Add the turkey and brown until it is separated into small pieces. (Ground turkey tends to stick together more than ground beef.) Drain off the fat. Add the tomato sauce, tomatoes, water, garlic, chile powder, paprika, oregano, cumin, and cayenne powder. Cover and simmer for 1 hour.

Add the beans and simmer for 1 hour. Stir in the cornmeal and simmer for 15 minutes more. Serve very hot.

Lean Sausage Chile

YIELD: 6-8 SERVINGS
TIME: 1 HOUR 30 MINUTES

4 tablespoons olive oil
2 pounds of three different types lean sausage links,
(Italian, chorizo, kielbasa, etc.)
2 cups coarsely chopped onions
2 cups coarsely chopped green bell peppers
4 cloves garlic, minced
12 ounces beer
2 cups crushed red tomatoes
2 cups tomato sauce
2 jalapeño peppers, seeded and chopped
4 cups cooked red kidney beans
Salt and freshly ground black pepper to taste

Remove the sausages from their casings. In a large pot, heat 2 tablespoons oil and brown the meat. Drain off the fat. Remove the sausage and set aside.

In the same pot, heat the remaining oil and sauté the onions, green peppers, and garlic until slightly soft. Add the beer and reserved sausage. Cook for 5 minutes, stirring frequently. Add the remaining ingredients and simmer, uncovered, for 1 hour. Serve.

Consuelo's Best Gazpacho

YIELD: 8-10 SERVINGS
TIME: 40 MINUTES PLUS CHILLING TIME

2-3 cloves garlic
3 cups tomato juice
2 tablespoons olive oil
2 tablespoons red wine vinegar
One 28-ounce can plum tomatoes *or* 6 large red tomatoes, chopped
3 small cucumbers, peeled and cut into 1-inch pieces
3 stalks celery, cut into 1-inch pieces
1 medium onion, cut into 1-inch pieces
4 tablespoons chopped fresh parsley *or* 2 tablespoons dried parsley
Herb croutons, for garnish
Diced cucumbers, for garnish

In a blender or food processor, finely chop the garlic. Add 1 cup tomato juice, oil, and vinegar and blend for 10 seconds.

Add *one half each* of the tomatoes, cucumbers, celery, onions, and parsley and blend until the vegetables are coarsely chopped, *not* pureed. Transfer the mixture to a 2-quart container.

Repeat with the remaining 2 cups tomato juice, cucumbers, celery, onion, and parsley. Cover and chill thoroughly. Serve icy cold with the croutons and diced cucumbers garnishing each serving.

Red Gazpacho

YIELD: 6-8 SERVINGS
TIME: 30 MINUTES PLUS CHILLING TIME

4 large red tomatoes, coarsely chopped
2 medium cucumbers, peeled and coarsely chopped
1 medium onion, coarsely chopped
1 medium green bell pepper, cored, seeded, and coarsely chopped
2 stalks celery, coarsely chopped
3 cups tomato juice
2 cloves garlic, minced
¼ cup red wine vinegar
2 medium red tomatoes, finely diced
1 small cucumber, peeled and finely diced
1 medium green bell pepper, cored, seeded, and finely diced
4 scallions, finely diced
Salt and freshly ground black pepper to taste
Tabasco sauce to taste
Herb croutons, for garnish

In a blender or food processor, combine the coarsely chopped vegetables with ¼ cup tomato juice. Blend until smooth.

Pour the vegetable mixture into a large bowl. Stir in the remaining tomato juice and vinegar. Add the finely diced vegetables. Add the salt, pepper, and Tabasco sauce.

To make the soup thinner, add water and adjust the vinegar and seasoning. Cover and chill thoroughly. Serve icy cold, garnished with the croutons.

Speckled White Gazpacho

YIELD: 6-8 SERVINGS
TIME: 30 MINUTES PLUS CHILLING TIME

4 medium cucumbers, peeled and coarsely chopped
1 small onion, diced
1 clove garlic, minced
1 quart buttermilk
2 cups low-fat sour cream
2 tablespoons fresh lemon juice
2 teaspoons dried dill
4 medium red tomatoes, finely diced
1 bunch fresh parsley, finely chopped
1 medium green bell pepper, cored, seeded, and finely diced
1 small cucumber, peeled and finely diced
Salt and freshly ground black pepper to taste

In a blender or food processor, combine the coarsely chopped cucumbers, onion, garlic, and buttermilk. Blend until smooth. Pour the mixture into a large bowl and add the remaining ingredients. Mix well. Cover and chill thoroughly. Serve icy cold.

Spring Dandelion & Watercress Salad

YIELD: 4 SERVINGS
TIME: 50 MINUTES

3 tablespoons white wine vinegar
2 teaspoons honey
1 clove garlic, minced
¼ teaspoon freshly ground black pepper
¼ teaspoon ground mustard
4 slices lean bacon
2 teaspoons vegetable oil
¼ cup chopped onions
4 cups dandelion greens, trimmed, washed, and dried
1 bunch watercress, washed and dried
½ cup raisins
2 large red tomatoes, sliced
½ cup finely chopped scallions (include green tops)

In a small bowl, combine the vinegar, honey, garlic, pepper, and mustard. Set aside for 30 minutes.

In a large skillet, sauté the bacon until crisp. Drain off the fat. Remove and crumble the bacon. Set aside. In the same skillet, heat the oil and sauté the onions until tender. Add the reserved vinegar mixture and mix well. Remove from heat.

In a large serving bowl, combine the dandelion greens and watercress. Add the raisins to the vinegar mixture and sprinkle over the mixed greens.

Arrange the tomato slices on salad plates and mound a serving of the salad mixture on each tomato slice. Sprinkle with the scallions and reserved bacon. Serve immediately.

. . . .

Fennel, Leek & Tomato Salad

YIELD: 4 SERVINGS
TIME: 15 MINUTES

1 medium fennel bulb, finely sliced
2 medium leeks, very finely sliced (white part only)
4 small red tomatoes, sliced
4 tablespoons olive oil
1 tablespoon fresh lemon juice
Salt and freshly ground black pepper to taste

In a medium-size bowl, combine the fennel, leeks, and tomatoes. In a small bowl, combine the oil, lemon juice, salt, and pepper. Mix well. Pour the oil mixture over the vegetables. Toss to blend and serve.

Indian Tomato Salad

YIELD: 4 SERVINGS
TIME: 15 MINUTES

3 medium red tomatoes, quartered
1 small onion, finely diced
6 ounces plain low-fat yogurt
Pinch cayenne powder
½ teaspoon ground cumin
2 tablespoons finely chopped fresh mint
Salt and freshly ground black pepper to taste

In a medium-size serving bowl, combine the tomatoes and onion. In a small bowl, combine the yogurt, cayenne powder, cumin, and mint. Mix well. Add the salt and pepper.

Pour the yogurt mixture over the tomato mixture. Toss to blend and serve.

TO SUBSTITUTE FRESH HERBS FOR DRIED HERBS in a recipe, use 1 tablespoon minced fresh herbs for each ½ teaspoon of dried herbs the recipe called for. In dishes served hot, add fresh herbs during the last 15 minutes of cooking for best results; long cooking of fresh herbs reduces their flavors. In dips, chilled soups, and other cold foods, add the herbs several hours ahead so the flavors can blend. In salad dressings, however, fresh herbs have the best color and flavor if added no more than 15 minutes before serving time.

Tomato & Green Bean Salad

YIELD: 4 SERVINGS
TIME: 15 MINUTES

½ pound green beans, topped and tailed
3 medium red tomatoes, quartered
2 tablespoons chopped fresh parsley
5 ounces plain low-fat yogurt
1 tablespoon tahini (sesame seed paste)
1 tablespoon fresh lemon juice
1 clove garlic, minced
Salt and freshly ground black pepper to taste

In a small saucepan, cook the green beans in rapidly boiling water for 7 minutes, or until the beans are tender crisp. Cool rapidly under cold running water. In a medium-size serving bowl, combine the green beans with the tomatoes and 1 tablespoon parsley. Mix well.

In a small bowl, combine the yogurt, tahini, lemon juice, garlic, salt, and pepper. Mix well. Stir the yogurt mixture into the green bean mixture and garnish with the remaining parsley. Serve immediately.

Tabouli

YIELD: 6-8 SERVINGS
TIME: 1 HOUR

This salad is especially good for picnics because it stores and keeps well.

SALAD:

1½ cups water
1½ cups bulgur
2 cups minced fresh parsley
1 medium cucumber, peeled and diced
4 medium red tomatoes, diced
1 medium green bell pepper, cored, seeded, and diced
1 bunch scallions, diced (include green tops)
½ pound feta cheese, crumbled
1 cup black Greek olives

DRESSING:

¼ cup olive oil
½ cup fresh lemon juice
1 clove garlic, minced
½ cup fresh mint *or* 3 tablespoons dried mint
½ teaspoon salt
¼ teaspoon freshly ground black pepper

In a small saucepan, bring the water to a boil. Turn off the heat and add the bulgur. Cover and set aside for 15 minutes.

In a large serving bowl, combine all the other salad ingredients. In a blender or food processor, combine the dressing ingredients, blend for 1 minute, and set aside.

Uncover the pot and fluff the bulgur with a fork. Let sit until cool. Then mix the bulgur with the vegetables. Pour the dressing over everything and allow to sit for 15 minutes before serving.

. . . .

Sun-Dried Tomatoes & Rigatoni

YIELD: 6-8 SERVINGS
TIME: 20 MINUTES PLUS CHILLING TIME

●

½ cup olive oil
2 tablespoons red wine vinegar
2 cloves garlic, minced
Salt and freshly ground black pepper to taste
2 cups chopped red tomatoes
12 sun-dried tomato quarters (see pages 275-276)
12-ounces low-fat mozzarella cheese, cut into ¼-inch cubes
4 tablespoons chopped fresh basil
4 cups cooked rigatoni pasta

In a large bowl, combine the oil, vinegar, garlic, salt, pepper, and red tomatoes. Add the sun-dried tomatoes, cheese, basil, and pasta. Toss to blend and chill for 1 hour. Serve.

Moroccan Cooked Salad

YIELD: 4 SERVINGS
TIME: 15 MINUTES

Fresh cilantro is essential for this salad.

2 medium red tomatoes, quartered
2 medium onions, diced
1 small cucumber, unpeeled, sliced lengthwise, seeded, and cut into ¼-inch slices
1 medium red or green bell pepper, cored, seeded, and chopped
4 tablespoons water
3 tablespoons olive oil
2 tablespoons fresh lemon juice
2 cloves garlic, minced
Salt and freshly ground black pepper to taste
2 tablespoons chopped fresh cilantro leaves

In a large saucepan, combine the tomatoes, onions, cucumber, bell pepper, and water and simmer for 5 minutes. Drain and set aside.

In a small bowl, combine the oil, lemon juice, garlic, salt, and pepper. Mix well. In a medium-size serving bowl, combine the tomato mixture with the oil mixture. Add the cilantro and toss gently to blend. Serve.

Greek Picnic Salad

YIELD: 8 SERVINGS
TIME: 30 MINUTES PLUS MARINATING TIME

This salad can be served on a bed of crisp lettuce or stuffed in pita bread to make sandwiches.

SALAD:
6 medium red tomatoes, chopped
2 medium green bell peppers, cored, seeded, and diced
1 small red onion, diced
1 small cucumber, unpeeled and diced
½ cup chopped fresh parsley
½ cup sliced black olives
¼ pound feta cheese, crumbled
2 cups cooked cubed chicken or turkey (optional)

DRESSING:
1 cup olive oil
¼ cup fresh lemon juice
¼ cup white wine vinegar
1 tablespoon Dijon mustard*
Salt and freshly ground black pepper to taste
2 cloves garlic, minced

In a large serving bowl, combine all the salad ingredients. In a blender or food processor, combine all the dressing ingredients and mix well. Pour over the salad. Let the salad marinate for at least 30 minutes. Serve.

**Use three times the amount of prepared mustard* for ground mustard unless the prepared mustard is very sharp, then use only two times as much.

Presto Pesto Salad

YIELD: 6-8 SERVINGS
TIME: 20 MINUTES

SALAD:

12 cups fresh spinach
4 large red tomatoes, quartered
5 scallions, finely diced
1½ cups finely chopped cucumbers
½ cup grated Parmesan cheese
½ cup chopped walnuts

DRESSING:

1 cup olive oil
½ cup fresh lemon juice
3 cloves garlic, minced
3 tablespoons fresh basil *or* 3 teaspoons dried basil
Salt and freshly ground black pepper to taste

Wash and dry the spinach. Tear into bite-size pieces and place in a large salad bowl. Arrange the tomatoes on top of the spinach. Sprinkle the scallions, cucumbers, cheese, and walnuts on top.

In a blender or food processor, combine the oil, lemon juice, garlic, basil, salt, and pepper and blend for 2 minutes. Pour the dressing into a container and serve with the salad.

Antipasto Salad

YIELD: 6-8 SERVINGS
TIME: 1 HOUR

SALAD:

2 cups red cherry tomatoes, cut into halves
1 cup diced pepperoni
2 cups cooked diced ham
2 cups diced provolone cheese
2 stalks celery, diced on the diagonal
1½ cups cubed cucumbers
½ cup sliced black olives
½ cup sliced green olives
1 medium green bell pepper, cored, seeded, and chopped
10 pepperoncini peppers (hot Italian peppers), left whole
One 6-ounce jar marinated artichoke hearts (optional)
Lettuce, for garnish

DRESSING:

1 cup olive oil
½ cup red wine vinegar
Salt and freshly ground black pepper to taste
1 tablespoon minced fresh parsley
2 teaspoons Dijon mustard
1 clove garlic, minced

In a large bowl, mix all the salad ingredients, except the lettuce. In a blender or food processor, combine all the dressing ingredients. Blend until smooth.

Pour the dressing over the salad and marinate for at least 30 minutes. Serve on a bed of crisp lettuce.

Tomato Feta Salad

YIELD: 8 SERVINGS
TIME: 10 MINUTES PLUS MARINATING TIME

SALAD:

6 medium red tomatoes, sliced
1 medium cucumber, peeled and sliced
1 small red onion, sliced into rings
¼ pound feta cheese, crumbled
Fresh parsley, for garnish

DRESSING:

½ cup olive oil
⅓ cup red wine vinegar
¼ cup chopped fresh parsley
½ teaspoon dried basil
¼ teaspoon salt
¼ teaspoon freshly ground black pepper
1 clove garlic, minced
1 teaspoon honey or sugar

Arrange the tomato and cucumber slices on a lipped serving dish. Arrange the onion rings and feta cheese on top.

In a blender or food processor, combine the dressing ingredients and process until well blended. Pour over the salad.

Let the salad marinate for 45 minutes before serving. Garnish with the parsley.

Tomato Aspic Supreme

YIELD: 8-10 SERVINGS
TIME: 20 MINUTES PLUS CHILLING TIME

To unmold a gelatin salad, first wet your serving plate with cold water. Then, run warm (not hot) water into a large bowl or in the sink. Dip the mold into the water up to the depth of the gelatin for 15 seconds. Loosen the gelatin around the edge of the mold with the tip of a paring knife. Place the serving dish on top of the mold and carefully turn it over. Gently shake the mold until the gelatin comes loose. Lift off the mold. If the gelatin doesn't come out readily, repeat the process.

4 cups tomato juice or puree
⅓ cup red wine vinegar
3 teaspoons Worcestershire sauce
Dash Tabasco sauce or cayenne powder to taste
Salt and freshly ground black pepper to taste
2 cups low-fat sour cream
⅓ cup water
2 tablespoons unflavored gelatin
1½ cups diced mixed vegetables (carrots, celery, green bell peppers)
Salad greens, for garnish
Sliced black olives, for garnish

In a large bowl, using a wire whisk, mix the tomato juice, vinegar, Worcestershire sauce, Tabasco sauce, salt, pepper, and sour cream until smooth.

In a small saucepan, add the water and sprinkle the gelatin on the water and let sit for 2 minutes. Heat the gelatin on low heat, stirring constantly. When the gelatin is dissolved, pour the gelatin mixture into the tomato mixture and mix well.

Put the diced vegetables into a 6-cup mold and pour the tomato mixture on top. Chill until firm, at least 2 hours. When the mold is set, unmold onto a serving plate. Garnish with the salad greens around the aspic and put the olives on top. Serve.

. . . .

Tomato Aspic with 34 Variations

YIELD: 6 SERVINGS
TIME: 20 MINUTES PLUS CHILLING TIME

●

Aspic can be partially frozen and served as a refreshing first course.

2 tablespoons unflavored gelatin
4 cups tomato juice or puree
2 tablespoons fresh lemon juice
Dash Worcestershire sauce
Dash Tabasco sauce
Salt and freshly ground black pepper to taste
1-2 cups chopped food

In a large bowl, soak the gelatin in ½ cup tomato juice for 5 minutes. In a small saucepan, heat the remaining tomato juice, lemon juice, Worcestershire sauce, Tabasco sauce, salt, and pepper. Add to the softened gelatin and mix well. Add the chopped food. Pour the mixture into an oiled mold and chill until firm, about 2 hours. Unmold and serve.

Tomato aspic can also be chilled in a large flat baking dish. When the aspic is firm, unmold it in a single sheet. Cut the aspic in half lengthwise. Place a sheet of aspic on a serving platter and top with a vegetable salad. Slip the other sheet of aspic on top to make a lovely buffet sandwich salad.

VARIATIONS: Add any of these foods to the basic recipe.

Blanched asparagus
Diced cucumbers
Celery slices
Diced green bell peppers
Grated carrots
Sliced radishes
Blanched corn
Red onion slices
Bean sprouts
Zucchini cubes
Blanched cauliflower
Blanched broccoli florets
Blanched peas
Cooked chick-peas
Cooked lima beans
Sliced scallions
Low-fat cream cheese balls
Cheese cubes
Mushroom slices
Sliced green or black olives
1 teaspoon dried basil
1 teaspoon dried dill
1 teaspoon chopped fresh mint
Sliced hard-cooked eggs
2 tablespoons chopped fresh parsley
Baked ham
Baked turkey
Baked roast beef
Crumbled bacon
Cooked shrimp
Cooked oysters
Cooked white fish
Cooked salmon
Cooked tuna

Tomato Vinaigrette

YIELD: 1¾ CUPS
TIME: 5 MINUTES

1 medium red tomato, peeled and quartered
1 cup vegetable oil
¼ cup red wine vinegar
¼ cup fresh lemon juice
1 tablespoon Dijon mustard
½ teaspoon dried basil
2 cloves garlic, minced
Salt and freshly ground black pepper to taste

In a blender or food processor, combine all the ingredients. Mix until well blended. Store in a glass jar and refrigerate until ready to use.

Vermonter Sweet & Sour Dressing

YIELD: 2½ CUPS
TIME: 10 MINUTES

1 cup vegetable oil
1 cup tomato catsup
1 cup red wine vinegar
½ cup pure maple syrup or honey
1 teaspoon chile powder
1 teaspoon Worcestershire sauce
¼ teaspoon garlic powder

In a medium-size bowl, combine all the ingredients. Mix well. Store in a glass jar and refrigerate until ready to use.

VARIATION: To make a low-calorie version of this dressing, eliminate the oil and use half the vinegar, half the maple syrup, and half the seasonings. This oil-less version also makes a tasty marinade for beef, lamb, and chicken.

Tangy Tomato Dressing

YIELD: 3½ CUPS
TIME: 5 MINUTES

1 small lime
2 cups vegetable oil
1 cup red wine vinegar
½ cup tomato paste
1 tablespoon Dijon mustard
2 tablespoons fresh dill *or* 2 teaspoons dried dill
Salt and freshly ground black pepper to taste
1 tablespoon fresh lemon juice

Chop the lime, including the peel, into small pieces. In a blender or food processor, combine all the ingredients and blend until smooth and light orange in color. Store in a glass jar and refrigerate until ready to use.

Rosy Cream Dressing

YIELD: 2 CUPS
TIME: 10 MINUTES PLUS CHILLING TIME

This dressing also makes an excellent vegetable dip.

1 tablespoon sugar or honey
2 teaspoons Dijon mustard
1 teaspoon salt
Dash cayenne powder
1 cup vegetable oil
1 egg
1 cup tomato pulp or puree
3 tablespoons cornstarch
¼ cup red wine vinegar
1 teaspoon dried dill

In a large bowl, combine the sugar, mustard, salt, cayenne powder, oil, and egg. Mix well and set aside.

In a blender or food processor, combine the tomato pulp and cornstarch and blend until smooth. In a small saucepan, cook this mixture on medium heat until the sauce thickens, stirring constantly.

Pour the tomato mixture into the oil mixture and beat vigorously until the dressing is smooth. Store in a glass jar and refrigerate until ready to use.

Speedy Chile Dressing

YIELD: 1 CUP
TIME: 5 MINUTES

Use this dressing on cooked green beans, snow peas, cauliflower, or broccoli.

2 cooked plum tomatoes, peeled and crushed
4 tablespoons vegetable oil
2 teaspoons hot pepper sauce
2 teaspoons tamari or soy sauce

In a small bowl, beat together all the ingredients. Store in a glass jar and refrigerate until ready to use.

Broiled Tomatoes

YIELD: VARIABLE
TIME: 10 MINUTES

1 medium red or green tomato per person
1 teaspoon melted soft margarine or vegetable oil per person

Select 1 tomato per person. Cut in half horizontally. Brush with the melted butter. Broil the tomatoes on a low rack until the tops are browned but not burned, and the tomatoes are heated all the way through. Serve.

VARIATIONS: Try one of these variations.

Herbs and spices: Sprinkle ½ teaspoon of one of the following dried herbs or ground spices on each tomato before broiling: garlic, thyme, marjoram, oregano, rosemary, coriander, parsley, dill, chives, cumin, basil, chervil, tarragon, chile powder, or curry powder.

Breadings: Sprinkle bread crumbs or wheat germ on top of the tomatoes before broiling. Or, combine equal amounts of breading and cheese and sprinkle on top before broiling.

Cheeses: Sprinkle on top of each tomato half before broiling: Parmesan, low-fat cheddar, Swiss, blue cheese, feta, low-fat cream cheese, or any other cheese on hand.

Garnishes: Garnish before broiling with diced onion, crumbled bacon, sesame seeds, chopped scallions, or anchovies.

Sour cream topping: Broil the tomatoes until they are heated. Combine 2 tablespoons low-fat sour cream and 2 teaspoons prepared mustard. Spread the sour cream mixture on top of the tomatoes and broil until the topping is bubbly.

Stewed Tomatoes

YIELD: 6 SERVINGS
TIME: 20 MINUTES

1 tablespoon vegetable oil
10 large red tomatoes, coarsely chopped
1 teaspoon honey
Salt and freshly ground black pepper to taste
2 teaspoons cornstarch (optional)
2 tablespoons water (optional)

In a large saucepan, heat the oil and add the tomatoes and honey. Simmer gently for 15 minutes, or until the tomatoes are soft. Add the salt and pepper. To thicken the tomatoes, in a small bowl, combine the cornstarch with the water. Add to the tomatoes and cook until thick. Serve.

VARIATIONS: This dish lends itself well to variations. Here are some additions to the basic recipe.

Onions: Sauté 1 small or medium diced onion in the oil for 5 minutes. Add the tomatoes.

Garlic: Add 1 minced clove garlic to the tomatoes.

Herbs: Add 1½ teaspoons of these dried herbs: basil, thyme, marjoram, or tarragon; or add curry powder or ground cumin to the tomatoes.

Bread crumbs: Stir in ½-¾ cup cracker crumbs or wheat germ during the last few minutes of cooking time.

Cinnamon: Add ¼-½ teaspoon ground cinnamon and salt and pepper to taste.

Cheese: Pour the stewed tomatoes into a casserole dish. Sprinkle the top with grated Parmesan cheese or grated low-fat cheddar cheese and broil until bubbly.

Bacon: Sauté 3 slices lean bacon until crisp. Drain off the fat. Crumble the bacon into the tomatoes after the tomatoes are cooked.

Ham: Sauté cubes of ham with the tomatoes.

. . . .

Herbed Cherry Tomatoes

YIELD: 6 SERVINGS
TIME: 5 MINUTES

●

2-3 tablespoons butter or soft margarine
½ teaspoon dried basil
½ teaspoon dried thyme
1 clove garlic, minced
4 cups red cherry tomatoes
Salt and freshly ground black pepper to taste

In a large skillet, melt the butter and sauté the basil, thyme, garlic, and tomatoes for 2-3 minutes or until hot. Add the salt and pepper. Serve immediately.

VARIATION: Sauté 2 tablespoons chopped fresh parsley for 5 minutes. Add the tomatoes, salt, and pepper.

Deviled Tomatoes

YIELD: 4 SERVINGS
TIME: 20 MINUTES

4 large red tomatoes, halved
Salt and freshly ground black pepper to taste
Cayenne powder to taste
½ cup bread crumbs
2 tablespoons butter or soft margarine
1 teaspoon Dijon mustard
¼ teaspoon Tabasco sauce
1 tablespoon Worcestershire sauce
2 teaspoons sugar
3 tablespoons cider vinegar
2 tablespoons unbleached all-purpose flour

Arrange the tomato halves in a shallow baking dish cut side up. Lightly sprinkle the tomatoes with salt, pepper, cayenne powder, and bread crumbs.

In a small saucepan, combine the remaining ingredients, except the flour, and stir on medium heat until the butter is melted. Sprinkle the flour over the butter mixture and stir until blended.

Spoon the butter mixture on top of the tomatoes. Broil for 10 minutes, or until the top is browned and bubbly. Serve.

Scalloped Tomatoes

YIELD: 6 SERVINGS
TIME: 20 MINUTES

2 cups bread crumbs
2½ cups *Stewed Tomatoes* (see page 94)
1 tablespoon minced onions
Salt and freshly ground black pepper to taste
Sugar to taste
Dried herbs to taste: basil, oregano, or marjoram
2 tablespoons butter or soft margarine

Preheat oven to 350° F. Cover the bottom of an oiled baking dish with 1 cup bread crumbs. Add the tomatoes and onions. Season to taste.

In a small bowl, combine the remaining bread crumbs with the butter. Cover the tomato mixture with the crumb mixture. Bake for 15 minutes or until well browned. Serve.

Braised Leeks & Tomatoes

YIELD: 6 SERVINGS
TIME: 40 MINUTES

●

8 medium leeks
2 tablespoons butter or soft margarine
2 tablespoons vegetable oil
2 medium onions, sliced into rings
2 large tomatoes, peeled and chopped
Salt and freshly ground black pepper to taste
1 cup chicken broth
2 teaspoons chopped fresh dill, for garnish

Trim the leeks and remove the coarse upper leaves. Slit open lengthwise. Cut off all but 2½ inches of the green leaves and discard. Wash thoroughly to remove sand and grit. Drain and cut crosswise into three or four pieces.

In a large skillet, heat the butter and oil and sauté the onions until tender. Stir in the leeks and tomatoes. Add the salt and pepper. Pour the chicken broth over the tomato mixture. Simmer gently until the leeks are tender crisp. Garnish with the dill and serve.

Tomato & Spinach Frittata

YIELD: 2 SERVINGS
TIME: 25 MINUTES

●

1 tablespoon vegetable oil
2 medium red tomatoes, cut into thin wedges
1 cup fresh spinach *or* ½ cup frozen spinach, thawed and drained
1 cup cooked rotini pasta
4 large eggs, beaten
2 tablespoons water
½ teaspoon freshly ground black pepper
½ cup grated Parmesan or Romano cheese

In a large skillet, heat the oil and sauté the tomatoes and spinach for 2 minutes. Add the pasta and cook for 8 minutes.

In a medium-size bowl, mix the eggs, water, pepper, and cheese. Pour the egg mixture over the tomato mixture, cover, and cook for 5 minutes, or until the eggs are set. Serve immediately.

Italian Green Beans with Sun-Dried Tomatoes

YIELD: 4 SERVINGS
TIME: 20 MINUTES

5 tablespoons olive oil
½ cup chopped onions
1 clove garlic, minced
16 sun-dried tomato quarters (see pages 275-276)
One 10-ounce package frozen Italian green beans
Salt and freshly ground black pepper to taste

In a large saucepan, heat the oil and sauté the onions and garlic until tender. Stir in the tomatoes and set aside.

Prepare the green beans according to package directions. Drain and add the green beans to the tomato mixture. Heat through and add the salt and pepper. Serve.

Corn & Tomatoes

YIELD: 6 SERVINGS
TIME: 30 MINUTES

This is a quick way to use surplus garden tomatoes and leftover corn on the cob. Serve over rice with broiled bluefish, cod, or halibut steaks.

2 tablespoons olive or vegetable oil
1 large red onion, very thinly sliced
2 cloves garlic, minced
6 large red tomatoes, cut into wedges
¼ cup chopped fresh basil *or* 1 tablespoon dried basil
3 cups cooked whole kernel corn
Cooked rice

In a large skillet, heat the oil and sauté the onion and garlic for 5 minutes. Add the tomatoes and basil. Stir well. Cover and simmer for 15 minutes.

Stir in the corn, cover, and cook 5 minutes more. Serve over the rice.

Chile Corn Fry-up

YIELD: 6-8 SERVINGS
TIME: 30 MINUTES

2 tablespoons vegetable oil
1 medium onion, diced
1 clove garlic, minced
1 medium red bell pepper, cored, seeded, and diced
1 medium green bell pepper, cored, seeded, and diced
2 cups whole kernel corn, fresh or frozen
4 medium red tomatoes, diced
2 tablespoons chile powder
Salt and freshly ground black pepper to taste

In a large skillet, heat the oil and sauté the onion and garlic for 5 minutes. Add the bell peppers and continue cooking for 5 minutes. Add the remaining ingredients and cook, uncovered, for 5-10 minutes, or until the tomatoes are soft. Serve hot.

Spiced Green Beans

YIELD: 8 SERVINGS
TIME: 30 MINUTES

●

2 tablespoons vegetable oil
1 medium onion, diced
2 cloves garlic, minced
6 medium red tomatoes, diced
4 cups green beans, diced
2 teaspoons ground cinnamon
½ teaspoon ground allspice
Salt and freshly ground black pepper to taste

In a large skillet, heat the oil and sauté the onion and garlic for 5 minutes. Add the remaining ingredients. Cook for 20 minutes, or until the beans are tender. Serve hot.

North End Beans

YIELD: 6 SERVINGS
TIME: 1 HOUR

●

½ cup water
Two 10-ounce packages frozen lima beans
2 tablespoons vegetable oil
1 small onion, diced
2 cloves garlic, minced
1 teaspoon dried basil
1 teaspoon dried oregano
1 teaspoon dried thyme
2 cups tomato juice or puree
½ pound provolone cheese, grated

Preheat oven to 350° F. In a small saucepan, boil the water and add the lima beans. Cook for 5-10 minutes, or until the beans are barely defrosted. Drain and set aside.

In a medium-size saucepan, heat the oil and sauté the onion and garlic for 5 minutes. Add the basil, oregano, thyme, tomato juice, and reserved beans. Pour this mixture into an oiled baking dish. Sprinkle the cheese on top. Bake for 35 minutes. Serve hot.

Green Beans Niçoise

YIELD: 4-6 SERVINGS
TIME: 35 MINUTES

●

1 pound green beans, topped and tailed
½ cup olive oil
2 shallots, minced
1 clove garlic, minced
2 medium red tomatoes, chopped
½ cup chopped celery
1 teaspoon salt
Freshly ground black pepper to taste
1 cup chicken broth
1 teaspoon minced fresh oregano
1 teaspoon minced fresh basil
1 tablespoon chopped fresh parsley

In a medium-size saucepan, cook the green beans in water until tender crisp. Drain and set aside.

In a large saucepan, heat the oil and sauté the shallots and garlic until soft. Add the tomatoes, celery, salt, pepper, and chicken broth. Simmer, uncovered, for 20 minutes.

Stir in the herbs and reserved beans. Simmer until heated through. Serve.

Quick Creamy Tomato Crunch

YIELD: 6 SERVINGS
TIME: 1 HOUR

●

2 tablespoons vegetable oil
1 large onion, sliced
4 stalks celery, diced
6 large red tomatoes, sliced
1 cup bread crumbs
3 tablespoons fresh basil *or* 3 teaspoons dried basil
Salt and freshly ground black pepper to taste
2 cups low-fat sour cream

Preheat oven to 350° F. In a medium-size skillet, heat the oil and sauté the onion and celery for 10 minutes.

In an oiled baking dish, arrange half of the tomato slices in the bottom of the dish. Sprinkle half of the bread crumbs on top. Spread the onion mixture on top of the bread crumbs and sprinkle with half of the basil, salt, and pepper. Cover with another layer of tomato slices. Sprinkle with the remaining basil. Spread the sour cream on top. Cover with the remaining bread crumbs. Bake for 30 minutes. Serve immediately.

Savory Red Tomato Crisp

YIELD: 6-8 SERVINGS
TIME: 1 HOUR 30 MINUTES

2 cups bread crumbs
½ cup melted butter or soft margarine
1 tablespoon dried oregano
2 eggs, beaten
1 teaspoon salt
2 tablespoons butter or soft margarine
1 small onion, chopped
1 clove garlic, minced
1 medium green bell pepper, cored, seeded, and chopped
2 cups chopped zucchini
6 large red tomatoes, chopped
1 tablespoon chile powder
Salt and freshly ground black pepper to taste
1 pound low-fat cheddar cheese, grated

Preheat oven to 350° F. In a large bowl, combine the bread crumbs, ½ cup butter, oregano, eggs, and salt. Press half the bread crumb mixture into the bottom of a 9 by 13-inch baking dish.

In a large skillet, melt the 2 tablespoons butter and sauté the onion, garlic, green pepper, and zucchini until tender crisp. Add the tomatoes and cook for 5 minutes. Drain off most of the liquid.

Add the chile powder, salt, and pepper to the vegetables and spread the vegetable mixture on the crust. Cover with the cheese. Sprinkle on the remaining bread crumb mixture. Bake for 45 minutes. Serve hot.

Tomato Zucchini Tart

YIELD: 8 SERVINGS
TIME: 1 HOUR 30 MINUTES

CRUST:

2 cups grated raw potato
1 small onion, finely diced
1 egg, lightly beaten
¼ cup unbleached all-purpose flour
Dash salt

FILLING:

2 cups grated cheese (low-fat cheddar, Swiss, low-fat mozzarella, or provolone)
2 cups thinly sliced zucchini
3 large red tomatoes, sliced
1 teaspoon dried basil
1 teaspoon dried oregano
½ teaspoon garlic powder
Salt and freshly ground black pepper to taste
1 small onion, diced

Preheat oven to 350° F. After grating the potato, squeeze out as much of the liquid as possible. Combine the potato with the onion, egg, flour, and salt. Mix well. Press the potato mixture into a well-oiled 9-inch pie pan. Bake for 30 minutes.

When the crust has browned around the edge a bit, remove from oven. Layer half of the cheese in the crust. Alternate layers of zucchini slices, cheese, and tomatoes. Sprinkle on the basil, oregano, garlic powder, salt, pepper, and onion. Top with the remaining cheese. Bake for 45 minutes, or until the top is golden brown. Serve.

Colache

YIELD: 4-6 SERVINGS
TIME: 1 HOUR

4 tablespoons vegetable oil
3 medium zucchini, cut into ¼-inch slices
1 large onion, thinly sliced
2 medium green bell peppers, cored, seeded, and chopped
4 medium red tomatoes, chopped
1¾ cups whole kernel corn, fresh or frozen
Salt and freshly ground black pepper to taste
Dash Tabasco sauce

In a large saucepan, heat the oil and sauté the zucchini until slightly browned. Remove from the saucepan and set aside.

In the same saucepan, add the onion and green pepper and sauté briefly. Add the tomatoes and corn and stir well. Mix in the salt, pepper, and Tabasco sauce. Cover and cook for 30 minutes. Uncover and cook 15 minutes more. Serve.

Ratatouille

YIELD: 8 SERVINGS
TIME: 45 MINUTES

This dish freezes well. Leftovers can be thawed and served, or incorporated into sauces and soups.

3 tablespoons olive oil
1 large onion, sliced
2 cloves garlic, minced
1 large eggplant, unpeeled and diced
1 medium zucchini, diced
2 medium green bell peppers, cored, seeded, and diced
5 medium red tomatoes, diced
1 teaspoon dried basil
1 teaspoon dried oregano
1 teaspoon dried thyme
1 teaspoon dried marjoram
1 cup tomato paste
Salt and freshly ground black pepper to taste
1 cup grated cheese (low-fat cheddar, Parmesan, or provolone), for garnish

In a large pot, heat the oil and sauté the onion and garlic until the onion is translucent. Add the eggplant and cook over medium heat for 5 minutes, stirring frequently. Add the remaining vegetables and herbs. Continue cooking for 10-15 minutes more, stirring frequently.

Add the tomato paste. If the sauce is too thick, add a bit of water. Add the salt and pepper. Cook for 5 minutes on medium heat. Serve immediately, passing the cheese as garnish.

Little Eggplant Pizzas

YIELD: 6-8 SERVINGS
TIME: 20 MINUTES

2 medium eggplants, unpeeled and cut into ½-inch slices
½ cup olive oil; reserve 1 tablespoon
1 small onion, diced
2 cloves garlic, minced
4 cups tomato juice or puree
½ teaspoon dried oregano
1 teaspoon dried basil
Dash dried thyme
2 tablespoons minced fresh parsley
Pinch rosemary, crumbled
1 teaspoon honey
Salt and freshly ground black pepper to taste
1 cup grated Parmesan cheese

Place the eggplant slices on a baking sheet. Brush each slice with the oil and broil until the eggplant is golden brown. Turn the slices over, brush with oil, and broil until golden.

In a large saucepan, heat 1 tablespoon of oil and sauté the onion and garlic. Add the tomato juice, herbs, honey, salt, and pepper. Simmer for 10-15 minutes.

Carefully spread the tomato mixture on each eggplant slice. Sprinkle with the cheese and broil for 5 minutes, or until the cheese is bubbly and the eggplant is heated through. Serve.

Calzones

YIELD: 12 SERVINGS
TIME: 2 HOURS 30 MINUTES

If you are cooking for a small group, freeze the leftovers for another meal.

3 tablespoons active dry yeast
2 cups warm water
1 tablespoon honey
1 teaspoon salt
5 cups unbleached all-purpose flour
1 medium head broccoli, chopped and steamed
1 pound low-fat ricotta cheese
1 small onion, finely minced
¾ cup grated Parmesan cheese
Salt and freshly ground black pepper to taste
4 cups *Italian Sauce* (see page 123)
12 slices low-fat mozzarella cheese
12 slices cooked ham

In a medium-size bowl, combine the yeast, water, and honey. Let sit for 5 minutes. Add the salt and 2½ cups flour and stir to form a smooth dough. Add the remaining flour and mix well. Place the dough on a floured surface and knead for 10 minutes. Cover and put in a warm place for 1 hour.

In a large bowl, combine the broccoli, ricotta cheese, onion, Parmesan cheese, salt, and pepper.

When the dough has risen, punch it down and divide into 12 pieces. Roll each piece into a 6-inch circle. Spoon ½ cup of the broccoli mixture into each circle. Top with a small amount of *Italian Sauce*, 1 slice mozzarella cheese, and 1 slice ham. Moisten the edge of the circle with water and fold the dough over to make a pocket. Crimp the edge.

Bake the calzones on an oiled baking sheet for 20 minutes or until browned. Serve with warm *Italian Sauce* to spoon over the calzones.

. . . .

Jerusalem Artichokes a la Provençale

YIELD: 4 SERVINGS
TIME: 35 MINUTES

1½ pounds Jerusalem artichokes
Water
2 tablespoons vegetable oil
1 clove garlic, crushed
2 teaspoons minced fresh parsley
1 large red tomato, chopped

Peel the artichokes. In a large pot of water, parboil the artichokes for 25 minutes. Drain and cut into bite-size pieces.

In a large skillet, heat the oil and sauté the garlic, parsley, and artichoke pieces until tender. Add the tomato and stir together. Serve hot.

Crêpes

YIELD: 12-16 CRÊPES
TIME: 45 MINUTES

2 eggs, beaten
1 cup low-fat milk
1 cup unbleached all-purpose flour
Dash salt
1 tablespoon vegetable oil

In a large bowl, mix all the ingredients together and beat with an electric mixer until the batter is completely smooth. Let sit for 30 minutes. This batter will be thin, similar to cream.

Make your filling. (See pages 115-116.)

When it's time to cook the crêpes, heat a small nonstick skillet or omelette pan and melt a teaspoon of butter or soft margarine in the pan. Spread the butter around to cover the whole bottom of the pan and part way up the sides. Pour a little less than a ¼ cup of batter into the pan and quickly tip the pan, moving it in a circular fashion to evenly spread the batter over the bottom and part of the sides of the pan. Cook the crêpe on medium heat for 2 minutes, then flip it over and continue cooking for 30 seconds more. Remove the crêpe to a plate and fill. Serve warm.

Italian Crêpes

YIELD: 16 CRÊPES
TIME: 1 HOUR PLUS TIME TO MAKE THE CRÊPES AND SAUCE

¼ cup vegetable oil
½ pound fresh mushrooms, sliced
1 medium onion, diced
3 cloves garlic, minced
4 pounds fresh spinach *or* 2 pounds frozen spinach, thawed and drained
2 cups low-fat ricotta cheese
1 pound low-fat mozzarella cheese, grated
16 crêpes (see page 114)
3 cups *Italian Sauce* (see page 123)

Preheat oven to 350° F. In a large skillet, heat the oil and sauté the mushrooms, onion, and garlic until limp. Transfer to a large bowl. In a large saucepan, steam the spinach until limp. Drain well and add to the mushroom mixture. Add the ricotta cheese and half of the mozzarella cheese.

Spoon ½ cup of the filling into each crêpe. Roll each crêpe and place in a baking pan. Spoon *Italian Sauce* over the filled crêpes and sprinkle the remaining mozzarella cheese on top. Bake for 30 minutes and serve immediately.

Spanish Crêpes

YIELD: 12 CRÊPES
TIME: 1 HOUR 30 MINUTES PLUS TIME TO MAKE THE CRÊPES

CHEESE SAUCE:

½ cup butter or soft margarine
½ cup unbleached all-purpose flour
2 cups low-fat milk
1 pound low-fat cheddar cheese, shredded
1 tablespoon Dijon mustard
Dash Worcestershire sauce
Salt and freshly ground black pepper to taste

CRÊPES:

¼ cup vegetable oil
1 large onion, diced
1 clove garlic, minced
1 cup uncooked diced pork
2 cups cooked diced ham
5 large red tomatoes, diced
¼ cup unbleached all-purpose flour
1 cup beef broth
Salt and freshly ground black pepper to taste
12 crêpes (see page 114)

In a large saucepan, melt the butter. Stir in the flour. Slowly add the milk, a little at a time, stirring after each addition to prevent lumps. Add the cheese, mustard, Worcestershire sauce, salt, and pepper. Continue cooking until the sauce is thick and smooth. Set aside.

Preheat oven to 350° F. In a large skillet, heat the oil and sauté the onion and garlic until the onion is translucent. Add the pork and cook until lightly browned. Stir in the ham and tomatoes.

In a small bowl, make a paste with the flour and ½ cup beef broth. Stir the paste into the ham mixture. Add the remaining broth, salt, and pepper. Simmer until the mixture thickens. Cool slightly.

Spoon ½ cup of the filling into each crêpe. Roll each crêpe and place in a baking pan. Spoon the reserved cheese sauce over the filled crêpes. Bake for 20 minutes or until hot and bubbly. Serve immediately.

. . . .

Simple Basic Tomato Sauce

YIELD: 4 CUPS
TIME: 2-3 HOURS

There is a 1:1 ratio of pounds of tomatoes to cups produced. This recipe can be increased or decreased accordingly.

4 pounds red tomatoes

Peel the tomatoes (see page 280) and cut into quarters. In a large stainless steel or enameled pot, cook the tomatoes on medium heat for 2-3 hours, or until the tomatoes are very soft and most of the liquid has evaporated.

Strain through a large sieve or food mill. If a thicker sauce is desired, cook the tomatoes longer.

Tomato sauce can be frozen (see page 274).

Red Taco Sauce

YIELD: 4 CUPS
TIME: 45 MINUTES

Serve this sauce with nachos, chicken, or any Mexican dish.

2 tablespoons vegetable oil
1 medium onion, diced
1 medium green bell pepper, cored, seeded, and diced
2 stalks celery, diced
3 cloves garlic, minced
4 cups tomato sauce
2 tablespoons chile powder
½ teaspoon ground cumin
1 jalapeño pepper, finely diced (optional)
Cayenne powder to taste

In a large saucepan, heat the oil and sauté the onion, green pepper, celery, and garlic for 10 minutes. Add the remaining ingredients and season to taste. Simmer for 15 minutes. Serve.

Cocktail Sauce

YIELD: 2 CUPS
TIME: 35 MINUTES

Serve this sauce with shrimp and other seafood.

1½ cups tomato sauce or catsup
4 heaping tablespoons prepared horseradish
2 tablespoons fresh lemon juice
Dash Tabasco sauce
Salt and freshly ground black pepper to taste

In a medium-size bowl, mix all the ingredients and let sit for 30 minutes. Serve.

Sweet & Sour Sauce

YIELD: 2½ CUPS
TIME: 20 MINUTES

This sauce is excellent with stir-fried beef, pork, or chicken, and chicken wing appetizers.

1 cup tomato sauce
1 cup cider vinegar
¼ cup fresh lemon juice
1½ cups honey
1 tablespoon ground mustard
Dash Tabasco sauce
1 small green bell pepper, cored, seeded, and minced
Salt to taste
2 tablespoons water
2 tablespoons cornstarch

In a medium-size saucepan, combine all the ingredients, except the water and cornstarch. Cook for 10 minutes. In a small bowl, stir the water and the cornstarch together until smooth. Add to the tomato sauce. Cook for 10 minutes or until thick and clear. Serve.

Celery Tomato Sauce

YIELD: 5 CUPS
TIME: 45 MINUTES

This sauce is great with meat loaf and other beef dishes.

2 tablespoons vegetable oil
1 medium onion, finely diced
2 cups finely diced celery
4 cups tomato sauce
2½ teaspoons chopped fresh cilantro *or* 1 teaspoon ground coriander leaves
1 teaspoon dried dill
Salt and freshly ground black pepper to taste

In a medium-size saucepan, heat the oil and sauté the onion and celery for 5 minutes. Add the remaining ingredients and simmer for 30 minutes. Serve.

Indian Curry Sauce

YIELD: 4 CUPS
TIME: 15 MINUTES

This is a spicy sauce to serve over steamed vegetables, fish, or chicken.

2 tablespoons vegetable oil
1 medium onion, diced
1 stalk celery, diced
4 cups tomato sauce
2 tablespoons honey
3-4 tablespoons curry powder

In a medium-size saucepan, heat the oil and sauté the onion and celery for 10 minutes or until tender. In a blender or food processor, combine the remaining ingredients and blend for 30 seconds. Return the sauce to the saucepan and reheat. Serve.

Italian Sauce

YIELD: 4 CUPS
TIME: 45 MINUTES

2 tablespoons olive oil
1 small onion, diced
2 cloves garlic, minced
½ teaspoon dried thyme
½ teaspoon dried oregano
½ teaspoon dried basil
1 bay leaf
¼ cup minced fresh parsley
¼ cup grated Parmesan cheese
½ cup dry red wine
1 teaspoon sugar or honey
4 cups tomato sauce
Salt and freshly ground black pepper to taste

In a medium-size saucepan, heat the olive oil and sauté the onion and garlic for 5 minutes. Add the herbs and continue cooking for 2 minutes. Add the remaining ingredients and cook for 30 minutes. Remove the bay leaf. Serve over hot pasta.

VARIATION: To make an Italian meat sauce, sauté 1 pound of lean ground beef with the onion and garlic. Drain off the fat and continue cooking as the recipe specifies.

Andrea's Rosy Basil Sauce

YIELD: 2½ CUPS
TIME: 20 MINUTES

¼ cup butter or soft margarine
2 cloves garlic, minced
5 medium red tomatoes, chopped
1 cup coarsely chopped fresh basil leaves
¼ cup unbleached all-purpose flour
Salt and freshly ground black pepper to taste
¼ cup low-fat milk or half-and-half (optional)
Grated Parmesan or Romano cheese, for garnish

In a large saucepan, melt the butter. Add the garlic and sauté for 1 minute. Add the tomatoes and basil and sauté for 5 minutes more. In a blender or food processor, combine the tomato mixture and flour. Blend until smooth.

Return the sauce to the saucepan. Add the salt and pepper. Thin with the milk, if desired. Cover and cook on low heat for 10 minutes.

Serve over hot pasta with the cheese sprinkled on top.

Marinara Sauce

YIELD: 4 CUPS
TIME: 3 HOURS 40 MINUTES

2 tablespoons butter or soft margarine
2 tablespoons olive oil
3 cups finely chopped onions
3 cloves garlic, minced
One 28-ounce can plum tomatoes, undrained
½ cup tomato paste
½ cup grated carrots
¼ cup grated Parmesan cheese
1 teaspoon sugar
¼ teaspoon freshly ground black pepper
1 teaspoon dried basil
½ teaspoon dried oregano
1 bay leaf
¼ cup chopped fresh parsley
½ cup red wine
2 cups water

In a large saucepan, melt the butter with the oil. Cook the onions for 20 minutes until tender and golden. Add the garlic, tomatoes, tomato paste, and carrots. Simmer for 10 minutes, stirring occasionally.

Add the remaining ingredients and cook very slowly, uncovered, for 3 hours. Remove the bay leaf. Serve over hot pasta.

Herb Sun-Dried Tomato Sauce

YIELD: 2 CUPS
TIME: 25 MINUTES

One 16-ounce can crushed tomatoes
1 tablespoon minced sun-dried tomatoes (see pages 275-276)
3 scallions, thinly sliced (include green tops)
1 teaspoon olive oil
½ teaspoon dried oregano
½ teaspoon dried basil
1 bay leaf, crushed
Salt and freshly ground black pepper to taste

In a medium-size saucepan, combine the first six ingredients and cook on medium heat for 15 minutes. Reduce heat and add the salt and pepper. Continue cooking for 5 minutes more. Remove the bay leaf. Serve over hot pasta.

Vegetable Sauce

YIELD: 12 CUPS
TIME: 50 MINUTES

¼ cup olive oil
2 medium onions, chopped
4 large carrots, thinly sliced
4 green or red bell peppers, cored, seeded, and chopped
6 cloves garlic, minced
2 medium zucchini, sliced and julienned
½ pound fresh mushrooms, sliced
6 cups tomato sauce
½ cup red wine or apple juice (optional)
1 tablespoon dried oregano
1 tablespoon dried thyme
½ teaspoon freshly ground black pepper

In a large skillet, heat the oil and sauté the onions, carrots, bell peppers, and garlic for 10 minutes. Add the zucchini and mushrooms and cook for 5 minutes.

Stir in the tomato sauce, wine, oregano, thyme, and black pepper. Simmer, uncovered, for 20-25 minutes. Serve over hot pasta, or divide and freeze for later use.

Mushroom & Walnut Sauce

YIELD: 2½ CUPS
TIME: 15 MINUTES

2 tablespoons olive oil
3 cloves garlic, minced
4 scallions, sliced (include green tops)
½ pound fresh mushrooms, sliced
¼ cup chopped walnuts
1 cup tomato sauce
1 cup canned crushed tomatoes
1 tablespoon dried basil
¼ teaspoon freshly ground black pepper

In a large skillet, heat the oil and sauté the garlic and scallions for 30 seconds. Add the mushrooms and stir-fry for 1 minute. Stir in the walnuts and cook for 1 minute.

Add the tomato sauce, tomatoes, basil, and pepper. Cook for 5-10 minutes. Serve over hot pasta.

Curried Tofu Sauce

YIELD: 6 CUPS
TIME: 45 MINUTES

2 tablespoons olive oil
2 cups chopped onions
1 cup chopped carrots
1 cup chopped celery
2 cloves garlic, minced
2 teaspoons curry powder
One 28-ounce can crushed tomatoes
½ pound tofu, diced

In a large skillet, heat the oil and sauté the onions, carrots, celery, garlic, and curry powder for 10 minutes, stirring occasionally.

Add the tomatoes and tofu and cook on low heat for 20 minutes, stirring gently. Serve over hot pasta.

Zucchini & Tomato Sauce

YIELD: 6 CUPS
TIME: 40 MINUTES

1 tablespoon olive oil
1 medium onion, finely chopped
2 cloves garlic, minced
3 cups cooked chopped red tomatoes
1 tablespoon dried oregano
½ teaspoon freshly ground black pepper
4 small zucchini, chopped

In a large skillet, heat the oil and sauté the onion and garlic for 5 minutes. Add the tomatoes, oregano, and pepper and simmer for 15 minutes. Add the zucchini and cook for 10 minutes more.

In a blender or food processor, spoon half of the tomato mixture and puree. Remove from the blender and set aside. Repeat with the remaining half of the tomato mixture.

Combine the two halves of the tomato mixture and serve over hot pasta, or freeze half for later use.

Chicken Liver Sauce

YIELD: 2 CUPS
TIME: 35 MINUTES

¼ pound lean bacon, minced
1 small onion, minced
¼ cup minced fresh parsley
½ pound chicken livers, separated and quartered
¼ pound fresh mushrooms, thinly sliced
¼ cup marsala wine
½ cup tomato sauce
Salt and freshly ground black pepper to taste
½ teaspoon ground sage

In a medium-size bowl, mix together the bacon, onion, and parsley to make a paste. In a large skillet, sauté the bacon mixture for 5 minutes, stirring occasionally. Drain off the fat.

Add the chicken livers and mushrooms and cook on medium heat until the chicken livers are browned. Add the remaining ingredients and cook for 10 minutes. Serve over hot pasta.

Anchovy Sauce

YIELD: 3½ CUPS
TIME: 30 MINUTES

Soak the anchovies in cold water first to remove some of the salt, if desired.

2 tablespoons olive oil
4-6 cloves garlic, minced
1 medium green bell pepper, cored, seeded, and finely chopped
2 tablespoons chopped fresh parsley
2 tablespoons chopped fresh basil *or* 1 teaspoon dried basil
Two 2-ounce cans anchovy fillets
½ teaspoon freshly ground black pepper
3 cups tomato sauce

In a large skillet, heat the oil and sauté the garlic, green pepper, parsley, and basil for 5 minutes.

Drain the anchovies and mash them. Add the anchovies to the skillet with the black pepper and tomato sauce. Simmer for 20 minutes. Serve over hot pasta.

Pork Ragout Sauce

YIELD: 8 CUPS
TIME: 1 HOUR

½ pound lean ground pork
2 tablespoons olive oil
1 large onion, chopped
2 medium carrots, chopped
4 cloves garlic, minced
1 large red bell pepper, cored, seeded, and chopped
2 medium zucchini, chopped
3 cups tomato sauce *or* one 28-ounce can crushed tomatoes
½ cup chopped fresh parsley
2 teaspoons dried thyme
2 teaspoons dried oregano
½ teaspoon freshly ground black pepper

In a large skillet, crumble the ground pork and brown on low heat for 5 minutes. Drain off the fat and set aside.

In the same skillet, heat the oil and sauté the onion, carrots, and garlic for 10 minutes. Add the bell pepper and zucchini and cook for 5 minutes.

Return the reserved meat to the skillet with the tomato sauce and the remaining ingredients. Stir thoroughly and simmer for 25 minutes. Cover the skillet if a thinner sauce is desired. Serve over hot pasta.

Neapolitan Quiche

YIELD: 6 SERVINGS
TIME: 40 MINUTES

1 cup tomato sauce
1 clove garlic, minced
½ teaspoon dried oregano
1 teaspoon dried basil
Salt and freshly ground black pepper to taste
3 eggs
1 cup low-fat ricotta cheese
Whole wheat pastry for one 8-inch pie crust
½ cup grated Parmesan cheese

Preheat oven to 350° F. In a medium-size bowl, combine the tomato sauce, garlic, oregano, basil, salt, and pepper. Mix well. In a small bowl, beat the eggs with the ricotta cheese. Combine the two mixtures, blending well. Pour into the pie shell and sprinkle with the Parmesan cheese.

Set the pie pan on a baking sheet and bake for 30 minutes until puffed and firm. Let stand for 10 minutes before serving. Serve.

Tarragon Shrimp with Rotelle

YIELD: 4 SERVINGS
TIME: 25 MINUTES

2 tablespoons olive oil
2 shallots, chopped
2 cloves garlic, minced
2 teaspoons dried oregano
1 teaspoon dried tarragon
⅛ teaspoon cayenne powder
1¼ pounds medium shrimp, peeled, deveined, and cut in half
2 cups tomato sauce
1 cup sliced black olives
1 pound rotelle pasta

In a large skillet, heat the oil and add the shallots, garlic, oregano, tarragon, and cayenne powder. Stir together and immediately add the shrimp pieces. Coat with the herb mixture and cook for 1 minute, stirring frequently.

Add the tomato sauce and olives. Simmer for 10 minutes, stirring frequently.

Prepare the rotelle according to package directions. Drain and place the pasta in a warm serving bowl. Cover with the sauce and serve immediately.

Shrimp in Spicy Orange Sauce

YIELD: 4 SERVINGS
TIME: 1 HOUR

●

3 tablespoons vegetable oil
4 cloves garlic, minced
2 cups tomato sauce
¾ cup orange marmalade
Juice of ½ lemon
1 tablespoon chopped fresh gingerroot
Salt to taste
1½ pounds medium shrimp, peeled and deveined
Cooked rice

In a large saucepan, heat the oil and sauté the garlic for 10 minutes until golden, stirring frequently. Add the tomato sauce and cook on medium heat for 10 minutes.

Stir in the remaining ingredients, except the shrimp and rice, and cook for 15-20 minutes or until slightly thick. Add the shrimp and cook for 5-7 minutes, or until the shrimp are pink and firm. Serve over the rice.

Deep Sea Scallop Sauté

YIELD: 4 SERVINGS
TIME: 25 MINUTES

If desired, substitute the scallops with monkfish, cut into 2-inch chunks. This dish is excellent over rotini pasta or rice.

2 tablespoons olive oil
2 cloves garlic, minced
1 medium red bell pepper, cored, seeded, and cut into 1-inch pieces
1 small zucchini, julienned
6 scallions, sliced (include green tops)
1½ teaspoons grated lemon zest
½ teaspoon freshly ground black pepper
1½ cups tomato sauce
1 cup half-and-half
1 pound sea scallops
1½ cups cooked whole kernel corn
¼ cup chopped fresh parsley

In a large skillet, heat the oil and sauté the garlic, bell pepper, and zucchini for 3 minutes. Add the scallions, lemon zest, and black pepper and sauté for 2 minutes. Add the tomato sauce and half-and-half and cook for 3 minutes, or until the tomato mixture begins to bubble.

Add the scallops and corn and simmer for 5 minutes, or until the scallops are cooked through. Sprinkle each serving with the parsley. Serve.

Jambalaya

YIELD: 6-8 SERVINGS
TIME: 1 HOUR 10 MINUTES

4 tablespoons olive oil
1 pound lean smoked link sausage (kielbasa or chorizo)
1 cup chopped onions
1 cup chopped green bell pepper
1 cup chopped celery
4 cloves garlic, minced
1 pound cooked ham, diced
4 cups canned crushed tomatoes with juice
One 6-ounce can tomato paste
1 cup dry red wine
1 cup water
1 teaspoon dried thyme
2 bay leaves
1 teaspoon crushed red chile pepper
Salt and freshly ground black pepper to taste
1 cup uncooked white rice
1 pound large shrimp, peeled and deveined

In a large skillet, heat 2 tablespoons oil and sauté the sausage until evenly browned. Drain off the fat. Remove the sausage and when cool, cut into 1-inch-thick pieces. Set aside.

In the same skillet, heat the remaining oil and sauté the onions, green pepper, celery, and garlic for 8 minutes or until slightly wilted. Add the ham, tomatoes, tomato paste, wine, and water. Mix well. Add the thyme, bay leaves, chile pepper, salt, and black pepper. Bring to a boil. Add the rice and reduce heat. Simmer, covered, for 20 minutes.

Add the shrimp and the reserved sausage pieces and cook for 10 minutes more, or until the shrimp are pink. Remove the bay leaves and serve hot.

. . . .

Baked Fillet of Flounder

YIELD: 4 SERVINGS
TIME: 1 HOUR

Flounder is a lean fish, only 90 calories in a 4-ounce portion uncooked. Flounder is also marketed as fluke, lemon sole, and gray sole. This method of cooking flounder with tomatoes in a covered dish is actually poaching, which keeps fish tender and moist.

4 flounder fillets
1-2 tablespoons vegetable oil
6 medium red tomatoes, peeled and sliced
½ cup sliced onions
1½ tablespoons chopped fresh parsley
2 cloves garlic, minced
½ teaspoon dried oregano
Salt to taste
¼ teaspoon freshly ground black pepper
2 tablespoons butter or soft margarine

Preheat oven to 350° F. Rinse the fillets in cold water and dry on paper towels. Coat the inside of a baking dish with the oil. Place the fillets in the dish and spread the tomatoes and onions over the fish. Add the parsley, garlic, oregano, salt, and pepper. Dot with the butter.

Cover with aluminum foil and bake for 20-30 minutes, or until the fish is tender and no longer translucent. Serve immediately.

Paella Valenciana

YIELD: 4-6 SERVINGS
TIME: 1 HOUR

¼ cup vegetable oil
One 3-pound frying chicken, cut up and skinned
1 large onion, chopped
1 clove garlic, minced
1 cup uncooked white rice
¼ teaspoon saffron
Salt and freshly ground black pepper to taste
Dash Tabasco sauce
½ cup tomato juice or puree
2 cups chicken broth
12 cherrystone clams, unshelled
½ pound medium shrimp, peeled and deveined
1 pound lean hot or sweet link sausage, cooked and sliced
1 cup peas
Pimiento strips, for garnish
Fresh parsley, for garnish

In a large skillet, heat 2 tablespoons oil and sauté the chicken pieces until well browned. Drain off the fat. Remove the chicken and set aside.

In the same skillet, add the remaining oil and sauté the onion and garlic until soft. Add the rice and cook until the rice turns yellow. Add the saffron, salt, pepper, and Tabasco sauce. Mix well.

Add the tomato juice, chicken broth, and the reserved chicken. Cover and cook for 20 minutes, or until the rice is tender.

Add the clams, shrimp, and sausage. Continue cooking until the chicken is tender and the shrimp are cooked. Add the peas and cook for 5 minutes more. Garnish with the pimiento and parsley and serve.

. . . .

Fancy Chicken Pepperon

YIELD: 6 SERVINGS
TIME: 1 HOUR

½ cup vegetable oil
6 chicken breasts or chicken pieces, skinned
2 large onions, diced
2½ cups diced red and green bell peppers
2½ cups diced red tomatoes
2 cloves garlic, minced
1 teaspoon dried basil
Salt and freshly ground black pepper to taste
½ pound lean bulk sausage
1 tablespoon vegetable oil
½ pound fresh mushrooms, sliced
Cooked rice

Preheat oven to 350° F. In a large skillet, heat ¼ cup oil and brown the chicken on all sides. Drain off the fat. Remove the chicken to a deep baking dish and set aside.

In a medium-size saucepan, heat the remaining oil and sauté the onions and bell peppers until limp. Add the tomatoes, garlic, basil, salt, and black pepper. Cook for 15 minutes, stirring frequently. Pour the tomato mixture over the reserved chicken.

In the same skillet, brown the sausage and drain off the fat. Crumble the sausage over the chicken. Heat the 1 tablespoon oil and sauté the mushrooms. Spread the mushrooms over the chicken. Cover the baking dish and bake for 30 minutes. Remove the cover for the last 15 minutes. Serve with the rice.

. . . .

Chicken Victoria

YIELD: 6 SERVINGS
TIME: 1 HOUR

CHICKEN ROLL:

3 chicken breasts, boned, skinned, and split in half
6 slices smoked ham
6 slices Swiss cheese
1 egg
½ cup low-fat milk
1½ cups bread crumbs
4 tablespoons vegetable oil

SAUCE:

¼ cup butter or soft margarine
2 cloves garlic, minced
6 medium red tomatoes, chopped
¼ cup unbleached all-purpose flour
¼ cup half-and-half
Salt and freshly ground black pepper to taste

Preheat oven to 350° F. Place the chicken breasts between two pieces of wax paper and pound them with a meat mallet until the breasts are

½ inch thick. Place a piece of ham and a piece of cheese on top of each chicken breast and roll up the breast.

In a small bowl, beat the egg and milk together. Dredge the chicken roll in the egg mixture and then in the bread crumbs.

In a medium-size skillet, heat the oil and brown the chicken roll on both sides. If the chicken begins to unroll, hold it together with wooden toothpicks. (Remove the toothpicks before baking.) Place the chicken rolls in a baking dish and bake for 30 minutes.

In a medium-size saucepan, melt the butter and sauté the garlic for 1 minute. Add the tomatoes and cook for 10 minutes. In a blender or food processor, add the tomato mixture and the flour and blend until smooth. Return the tomato mixture to the saucepan, add the half-and-half, salt, and pepper. Keep warm on low heat until the chicken is baked.

Pour the tomato mixture over the chicken and serve.

Arroz con Pollo

YIELD: 4 SERVINGS
TIME: 1 HOUR 25 MINUTES

¼ cup vegetable oil
One 3-pound frying chicken, cut up and skinned
1 medium onion, chopped
1 medium green bell pepper, cored, seeded, and chopped
1 clove garlic, minced
½ cup uncooked white rice
2 cups tomato juice or puree
1 cup chicken broth
½ teaspoon saffron
Salt and freshly ground black pepper to taste
One 10-ounce package frozen peas
½ cup sliced olives, green or black
One 2-ounce jar pimiento pieces, for garnish
¼ cup chopped fresh parsley, for garnish

Preheat oven to 350° F. In a large skillet, heat 2 tablespoons oil and sauté the chicken pieces until golden. Drain off the fat. Remove the chicken to a deep baking dish and set aside.

In the same skillet, add the remaining oil and sauté the onion, green pepper, and garlic until soft. Add the rice and sauté for 3 minutes, stirring frequently. Add the tomato juice, chicken broth, saffron, salt, and pepper. Bring to a boil.

Pour over the chicken and bake for 40 minutes. Add the peas and olives and cook for 10 minutes more. Garnish with the pimiento and parsley and serve.

Chicken Stir-Fry

YIELD: 4-5 SERVINGS
TIME: 30 MINUTES

¼ cup tamari or soy sauce
¼ cup dry sherry
¼ cup water
2 tablespoons cornstarch
1 chicken breast, boned, skinned, and cut into 1-inch pieces
6 tablespoons vegetable oil
1 medium onion, sliced in rings
2 cloves garlic, minced
1 medium green bell pepper, cored, seeded, and coarsely diced
½ cup sliced water chestnuts
2 medium red tomatoes, cut into wedges
Cooked rice

In a small bowl, mix the tamari, sherry, water, and cornstarch to make a marinade for the chicken. Marinate the chicken in the marinade for 15 minutes.

In a wok or large skillet, heat 3 tablespoons oil and stir-fry the onion for 1 minute. Add the garlic, green pepper, and water chestnuts and stir-fry until the vegetables are tender crisp. Remove the vegetables and set aside.

Heat the remaining oil in the wok and add the chicken and marinade. Stir-fry for 5 minutes, or until the chicken is cooked. Add the reserved vegetables and the tomatoes and cook for 2 minutes, or until the tomatoes are warm. Serve with the rice.

Chicken Cacciatora

YIELD: 4 SERVINGS
TIME: 1 HOUR

One 3-pound frying chicken, cut up and skinned
½ cup unbleached all-purpose flour
1 teaspoon salt
1 teaspoon ground paprika
¼ cup vegetable oil
2 tablespoons vegetable oil
2 cloves garlic, minced
1 small onion, chopped
1 medium carrot, chopped
1 stalk celery, chopped
¼ cup chopped fresh parsley
1 bay leaf
2 cups tomato sauce
½ cup dry white wine
Cooked pasta

Dredge the chicken with the flour mixed with the salt and paprika. In a large skillet, heat the ¼ cup oil and brown the chicken on all sides. Drain off the fat. Remove the chicken and set aside.

In the same skillet, heat the 2 tablespoons oil and sauté the garlic, onion, carrot, and celery until soft. Add the parsley, bay leaf, and tomato sauce. Bring to a boil. Add the reserved chicken and wine. Reduce heat and simmer, covered, for 30 minutes. Remove the bay leaf. Serve over hot pasta.

Chicken Enchiladas

YIELD: 4 SERVINGS
TIME: 40 MINUTES

1 pound chicken breasts, boned and skinned
¼ cup tomato juice
6 tablespoons low-fat cream cheese
2 tablespoons *Salsa* (see page 41)
1 tablespoon vegetable oil
1 small onion, chopped
3 cloves garlic, minced
One 28-ounce can crushed tomatoes
One 3½-ounce can green chile peppers, chopped
1 teaspoon ground coriander
¼ cup vegetable oil
8 soft corn tortillas
1½ cups low-fat sour cream
¼ cup chopped fresh chives

Preheat oven to 400° F. In a large skillet, combine the chicken and tomato juice. Cover and simmer for 10 minutes. Reserve ⅓ cup of the liquid. Thinly slice the chicken and set aside.

In a medium-size bowl, blend together the cream cheese, reserved liquid, and *Salsa*. Stir in the reserved chicken.

In the same skillet, heat the 1 tablespoon oil and sauté the onion and garlic for 2 minutes. Add the tomatoes, chile peppers, and coriander and simmer for 5 minutes.

In a medium-size skillet, heat the ¼ cup oil and drop each tortilla into the hot oil for 10 seconds. Remove immediately to a 9 by 12-inch baking dish and spoon 2-3 tablespoons of the chicken mixture along the center of each tortilla. Roll up and place seam-side down in the baking dish. Repeat until all the tortillas and the filling have been used.

Spoon the tomato mixture over the filled tortillas and bake for 15 minutes. In a small bowl, mix the sour cream and chives and spoon over each cooked tortilla. Serve hot.

. . . .

Italian Chicken Casserole

YIELD: 8-10 SERVINGS
TIME: 1 HOUR 45 MINUTES

Turkey can be substituted for the chicken.

8 ounces macaroni pasta
5 cups tomato sauce
1½ teaspoons chopped fresh basil *or* ½ teaspoon dried basil
1½ teaspoons chopped fresh oregano *or* ½ teaspoon dried oregano
1 tablespoon chopped fresh parsley
1 clove garlic, minced
1 small onion, minced
1 tablespoon olive oil
½ cup grated provolone cheese
1 pound low-fat ricotta cheese
Dash nutmeg
Salt to taste
2 eggs
1 cup cooked finely chopped chicken
5 small zucchini, sliced

Prepare the macaroni according to package directions until slightly cooked. Drain and set aside.

Preheat oven to 350° F. In a small saucepan, mix together the tomato sauce, basil, oregano, parsley, garlic, onion, and oil. Simmer for 15 minutes. In a large bowl, combine the cheeses, nutmeg, and salt. Beat in the eggs. Stir in the chicken.

Spread 2 cups of the tomato mixture in a large oiled casserole dish. Layer the reserved pasta over the tomato mixture. Cover with a layer of zucchini. Pour the chicken mixture over the zucchini and the remaining tomato mixture over all.

Cover and bake for 1 hour 30 minutes or until bubbly. Serve immediately.

Stofado

YIELD: 6 SERVINGS
TIME: 3-4 HOURS

2 chicken breasts, skinned and split in half
4 chicken thighs, skinned
4 tablespoons vegetable oil
Salt and freshly ground black pepper to taste
4 large onions, halved
1 bay leaf
1 teaspoon dried thyme
¼ cup chopped fresh parsley
5 cloves garlic, crushed
2 cups tomato sauce
½ cup chopped walnuts, for garnish
¼ cup crumbled feta cheese, for garnish

Preheat the broiler. Place the chicken on a baking sheet and brush with the oil. Broil four inches away from the heat until golden. Turn and brush with the oil. Broil the undersides until golden. Place the chicken in a deep baking dish. Add the salt and pepper.

Preheat oven to 275° F. In a large saucepan, cover the onions with water and bring to a boil. Boil for 5 minutes. Drain and add the onions to the baking dish.

In a small bowl, combine the bay leaf, thyme, parsley, garlic, and tomato sauce. Pour the tomato mixture over the chicken and onions. Cover and bake for 3-4 hours, stirring every 30 minutes. Remove the bay leaf. Garnish each serving with the walnuts and cheese. Serve.

Chicken Livers Hunter Style

YIELD: 4 SERVINGS
TIME: 50 MINUTES

●

4 tablespoons olive oil
1½ cups chopped red bell peppers
4 cloves garlic, minced
⅔ cup chopped scallions (include green tops)
½ pound fresh mushrooms, sliced
½ cup chopped fresh parsley
¼ cup chopped fresh oregano
½ teaspoon freshly ground black pepper
¼ teaspoon hot red pepper flakes
1 pound chicken livers, separated and cut in half
3 cups chopped red tomatoes
½ cup tomato sauce
1 pound cooked linguine pasta
½-1 cup grated Romano cheese

In a large skillet, heat 2 tablespoons oil and sauté the bell peppers, garlic, and scallions for 3 minutes. Stir in the mushrooms, parsley, oregano, black pepper, and pepper flakes. Cook for 2 minutes. Remove the mixture and set aside.

In the same skillet, heat the remaining oil and sauté the chicken livers for 3-4 minutes, stirring frequently. Stir in the tomatoes and the reserved mixture. Simmer for 20 minutes.

Prepare the linguine according to package directions. Drain and place on a warm serving platter. Pour the tomato mixture over the pasta and top with the cheese. Serve immediately.

Meat Loaf Maria Luisa

YIELD: 4 SERVINGS
TIME: 1 HOUR 10 MINUTES

¼ cup low-fat milk
½ cup tomato sauce
2 slices bread, crusts removed
1½ pounds lean ground beef
2 tablespoons minced onions
1 clove garlic, minced
1 tablespoon Worcestershire sauce
2 eggs
Salt and freshly ground black pepper to taste
½ cup grated Parmesan cheese
1 teaspoon dried oregano
½ teaspoon dried basil
1 cup low-fat ricotta cheese

Preheat oven to 350° F. In a small saucepan, heat the milk and ¼ cup tomato sauce. Add the bread and let stand until the bread is well soaked.

In a large bowl, mix together the ground beef, onions, garlic, Worcestershire sauce, eggs, and bread mixture. Add the salt and pepper and mix in ¼ cup Parmesan cheese. In a small bowl, mix together the oregano, basil, and ricotta cheese.

Put one third of the meat mixture into an oiled baking dish and shape into a rectangle. Spread with half of the ricotta cheese mixture. Layer with another third of the meat mixture and top with the remaining ricotta cheese mixture. Layer with the remaining meat mixture and cover with the remaining tomato sauce. Sprinkle the remaining Parmesan cheese over all and bake for 45 minutes. Serve hot.

Turkish Meatballs in Tomato Sauce

YIELD: 4 SERVINGS
TIME: 1 HOUR

½ cup cider
2 thick slices whole wheat bread
1 pound lean ground lamb
1 medium onion, finely chopped
2 tablespoons chopped fresh parsley
1 teaspoon ground paprika
Salt to taste
2 eggs
½ cup unbleached all-purpose flour
2 tablespoons butter or soft margarine
1 tablespoon vegetable oil
2 cups tomato sauce
Cooked rice pilaf

Preheat oven to 325° F. In a medium-size saucepan, heat ¼ cup cider and soak the bread in the cider for 3 minutes. Squeeze the bread dry. Set aside.

In a large bowl, combine the lamb, onion, parsley, paprika, salt, eggs, and the reserved bread. Mix together until well blended. Shape the meat into 1½-inch meatballs. Dust the meatballs with the flour.

In a medium-size skillet, heat the butter and oil and brown the meatballs on all sides. Drain off the fat. Remove the meatballs to a baking dish.

In a medium-size saucepan, add the tomato sauce and the remaining cider. Bring to a boil, stirring frequently. Pour the tomato mixture over the meatballs and bake for 30 minutes. Serve over the rice pilaf.

Tomato Marinated Steak

YIELD: 4 SERVINGS
TIME: 30-40 MINUTES PLUS MARINATING TIME

•

To marinate the meat, place the meat and the marinade in a sealable plastic bag large enough for the meat to lie flat. Using a plastic bag for marinating makes turning the meat easy and clean-up a snap.

1½ cups tomato juice
½ cup fresh lemon juice
⅓ cup tamari or soy sauce
4 cloves garlic, coarsely chopped
½ teaspoon freshly ground black pepper
⅛ teaspoon ground ginger
1 tablespoon sugar
1½-2 pounds london broil or flank steak
1-2 tablespoons cornstarch

In a medium-size bowl, make a marinade by combining all the ingredients, except the meat and the cornstarch. Pierce the meat in several places with a sharp knife. Cover the meat with the marinade and refrigerate for 5-6 hours or overnight, turning occasionally.

Preheat the broiler. Remove the meat and reserve the marinade. Broil the steak for 8-10 minutes on each side, or until the steak is cooked to preference.

In a medium-size saucepan, mix a small amount of the marinade with the cornstarch until smooth. Gradually add the remaining marinade and cook over low heat, stirring until thick. Cut the steak on the diagonal into thin slices. Pour the sauce over the steak and serve immediately.

Pot Roast Dinner

YIELD: 6-8 SERVINGS
TIME: 4-5 HOURS

2-3 pounds beef roast
2 cups water
4 medium carrots, quartered
4 medium potatoes, quartered
2 stalks celery, quartered
4 small onions
2 tablespoons minced fresh parsley
Salt and freshly ground black pepper to taste
4 cups chopped red tomatoes
1½ cups cooked lima beans

Heat a large pot until a drop of water sizzles on the surface. Sear the roast on all sides. Add the water. Lower the heat, cover, and cook for 2 hours.

Add the carrots, potatoes, celery, and onions. Stir in the parsley, salt, pepper, and tomatoes. Cover and cook for 1-2 hours, or until the vegetables are tender.

Add the lima beans and cook until heated through. Arrange the vegetables and meat on a warmed platter. Pour the pan juices into a gravy pitcher and serve with the meat.

Tenderloin of Pork with Fusilli and Tomato Sauce

YIELD: 4 SERVINGS
TIME: 40 MINUTES

⅓ cup olive oil
1 tablespoon red wine vinegar
2 cloves garlic, crushed
1 tablespoon dried oregano
1 tablespoon dried basil
1½ pounds lean pork tenderloin

FUSILLI AND SAUCE:
12 ounces fusilli pasta
1½ cups tomato sauce
½ cup half-and-half
3 cloves garlic, minced
⅛ teaspoon cayenne powder
1 tablespoon dried oregano

In a small bowl, mix together the oil, vinegar, garlic, oregano, and basil. Place the pork in a shallow dish and cover with the oil mixture. Marinate for 30 minutes, turning once.

Place the pork on the grill or under the broiler and cook six inches from the heat. Broil for 10 minutes. Turn and broil the underside for 10 minutes more. Slice the meat into ½-inch thick slices and drizzle with the remaining marinade.

Prepare the fusilli according to package directions. Drain and place on a warm serving platter.

In a medium-size saucepan, combine the remaining ingredients and cook on medium heat for 5 minutes or until hot. Cover the pasta with the tomato mixture and serve immediately with the pork slices.

. . . .

Mexican Strata

YIELD: 6 SERVINGS
TIME: 50 MINUTES

9 flat corn tostadas
1½ cups cooked red kidney beans
1½ cups whole kernel corn
1½ cups grated jalapeño Monterey Jack cheese
1 small onion, chopped
1 small green bell pepper, cored, seeded, and finely chopped
2 cups canned crushed tomatoes
2 cloves garlic, minced
½ teaspoon ground cumin
½ teaspoon chile powder

Preheat oven to 350° F. Break the tostadas in half and arrange six pieces on the bottom of an oiled casserole dish. Layer ½ cup each of the beans, corn, and cheese on the tostadas. Sprinkle with the onion and green pepper. Repeat the layers two more times.

In a small bowl, combine the tomatoes, garlic, cumin, and chile powder. Mix well. Pour over the layers and bake for 40 minutes. Serve hot.

Fettuccine Carrotine

YIELD: 4-6 SERVINGS
TIME: 1 HOUR

2 tablespoons vegetable oil
¼ cup minced onions
½ cup minced celery
1 cup grated carrots
2 cups chopped red tomatoes
2 cups tomato sauce
¼ teaspoon dried oregano
2 cloves garlic, minced
1 teaspoon sugar
Salt and freshly ground black pepper to taste
12 ounces fettucine pasta
6 tablespoons butter or soft margarine
¼ cup minced fresh parsley
½ cup grated low-fat sharp cheddar cheese

In a medium-size saucepan, heat the oil and sauté the onions, celery, and carrots until soft. Stir in the tomatoes, tomato sauce, oregano, and garlic. Bring to a boil. Add the sugar, salt, and pepper. Reduce heat and cover. Simmer for 30 minutes.

Prepare the fettuccine according to package directions. Drain and place in a warm serving bowl. Pour the tomato mixture over the pasta and top with the cheese. Serve immediately.

Potatoes & Broccoli in Cheesy Tomato Sauce

YIELD: 4-6 SERVINGS
TIME: 1 HOUR

6 medium potatoes
2 cups broccoli florets
2 tablespoons butter or soft margarine
1 tablespoon olive oil
4 scallions, chopped
3 medium red tomatoes, quartered
½ teaspoon ground cumin
½ teaspoon ground coriander
¼ teaspoon freshly ground black pepper
1 cup grated Grùyere or Swiss cheese

In a large saucepan, cover the potatoes with water and boil for 20 minutes or until tender. Drain and cool. Peel and quarter the potatoes. Place in an oiled baking dish in a warm oven. In a small saucepan, steam the broccoli until tender crisp. Add to the potatoes.

In a medium-size skillet, melt the butter with the oil and sauté the scallions for 2-3 minutes. Stir in the tomatoes, cumin, coriander, and pepper. Simmer for 10 minutes, or until the tomato mixture starts to thicken.

Add the cheese and cook until the cheese is melted, stirring frequently. Pour the tomato mixture over the potato mixture and serve warm.

Eggplant Parmesan

YIELD: 8-10 SERVINGS
TIME: 1½-2 HOURS

●

3 medium eggplants, cut into ¼-inch slices
Unbleached all-purpose flour
¼ cup vegetable oil
3 tablespoons vegetable oil
2 cloves garlic, minced
¼ cup chopped onions
2-3 tablespoons chopped fresh parsley
½ pound lean ground chuck
Salt and freshly ground black pepper to taste
3 cups tomato sauce
1 pound low-fat ricotta cheese
2 eggs, beaten
1 cup low-fat mozzarella cheese
¼ cup grated Parmesan cheese
12 fresh basil leaves

Dust the eggplant with the flour. In a large skillet, heat the ¼ cup oil and cook the eggplant on high heat until soft and light brown. (Add more oil if needed.) Drain on paper towels.

Preheat oven to 400° F. In the same skillet, heat the 3 tablespoons oil, and sauté the garlic and onions until soft. Add the parsley and ground chuck and sauté until the meat is browned. Add the salt and pepper. Drain off the fat.

Add the tomato sauce and simmer for 30 minutes, stirring occasionally. In a small bowl, combine the ricotta cheese and eggs. Blend well.

In a large baking dish, alternate layers of eggplant, ricotta cheese mixture, mozzarella cheese, Parmesan cheese, basil, and tomato mixture until all the ingredients are used. (Start and finish the layers with the tomato mixture.) Cover and bake for 30 minutes, or until the tomato mixture is bubbly and the eggplant is heated through. Serve immediately.

. . . .

Quick "Lasagna"

YIELD: 6 SERVINGS
TIME: 45 MINUTES

1 pound pasta shells
½ pound low-fat ricotta cheese
6 ounces low-fat mozzarella cheese
½ cup grated Parmesan cheese
5 cups tomato sauce

Preheat oven to 350° F. Prepare the shells according to package directions. Drain and set aside.

In a large bowl, combine the ricotta cheese, two-thirds of the mozzarella cheese, and ¼ cup Parmesan cheese. Mix in the reserved pasta and place in an oiled baking dish.

Pour the tomato sauce over the pasta shells. Sprinkle with the remaining cheeses and bake for 25 minutes. Serve.

Zucchini Moussaka

YIELD: 6-8 SERVINGS
TIME: 1 HOUR 30 MINUTES

2 pounds lean ground lamb
1 large onion, chopped
3 cloves garlic, minced
4 large red tomatoes, chopped
½ cup tomato sauce
¼ teaspoon chile powder
Salt and freshly ground black pepper to taste
½ teaspoon ground allspice
½ teaspoon ground cinnamon
1 tablespoon chopped fresh mint
½ pound Monterey Jack cheese, shredded
¼ cup vegetable oil
8 cups thickly sliced zucchini

Preheat oven to 350° F. In a large skillet, cook the ground lamb, onion, and garlic until the meat is browned and the onion is soft. Drain off the fat. Add the tomatoes, tomato sauce, chile powder, salt, pepper, allspice, cinnamon, and mint. Mix well. Bring to a boil. Reduce heat and simmer for 40 minutes. Remove from heat, stir in half the cheese, and set aside.

In another large skillet, heat the oil and sauté the zucchini until tender crisp. In a deep baking dish, layer the zucchini, reserved meat mixture, and remaining cheese. Repeat the layers, ending with the zucchini. Sprinkle any remaining cheese on top and bake for 30 minutes. Serve immediately.

Chicken & Spinach Lasagna

YIELD: 8-10 SERVINGS
TIME: 1 HOUR 30 MINUTES

1 cup grated Parmesan cheese
3 cups low-fat ricotta cheese
2 cups cooked chopped spinach
1 cup chopped fresh parsley
3 cloves garlic, minced
1½ teaspoons ground mace
½ teaspoon freshly ground black pepper
1 tablespoon dried oregano
1½ cups chopped red tomatoes
1 cup tomato sauce
12-16 cooked lasagna noodles
3 cups cooked thinly sliced chicken
2 cups grated low-fat mozzarella cheese
½ cup grated Romano cheese

Preheat oven to 350° F. In a large bowl, mix together the Parmesan cheese, ricotta cheese, spinach, parsley, garlic, mace, pepper, and oregano. In a small bowl, combine the tomatoes and tomato sauce.

Make a layer of noodles in an oiled 9 by 12-inch baking dish. Spread with one-third of the ricotta mixture, followed by one-third of the chicken, one-third of the tomato mixture, and one-third of the mozzarella cheese. Repeat the layers two more times.

Sprinkle the top with the Romano cheese and bake for 45 minutes, or until the center is steaming. Let stand for 10 minutes for easier cutting. Serve.

Garden Patch Lasagna

YIELD: 8 SERVINGS
TIME: 1 HOUR 20 MINUTES

2 cups chopped red tomatoes
1 cup tomato sauce
½ cup dry white wine
1 clove garlic, minced
½ teaspoon dried oregano
½ teaspoon dried basil
1 bay leaf
¼ teaspoon freshly ground black pepper
1 tablespoon butter or soft margarine
1 tablespoon olive oil
1 medium onion, chopped
½ pound fresh mushrooms, sliced
1 small carrot, finely chopped
1 small green bell pepper, cored, seeded, and chopped
1 stalk celery, chopped with leaves
½ pound cooked lasagna noodles
1½ cups grated Parmesan cheese
8 ounces low-fat mozzarella cheese slices
1 pound low-fat ricotta cheese

Preheat oven to 400° F. In a large saucepan, combine the tomatoes, tomato sauce, wine, garlic, oregano, basil, bay leaf, and black pepper. Simmer for 15 minutes and set aside. Remove the bay leaf.

In a large skillet, melt the butter with the oil and sauté the onion for 10 minutes until tender and golden. Stir in the mushrooms, carrot, green pepper, and celery. Cook until tender crisp, stirring frequently. Combine the reserved tomato mixture with the mushroom mixture and simmer for 15 minutes more.

Spoon a thin layer of the combined mixture over the bottom of an 8 by 12-inch baking dish. Arrange a layer of noodles on the bottom. Top with half of the Parmesan cheese. Layer with half of the mozzarella cheese slices. Top with half of the ricotta cheese. Spoon half of the combined mixture over the layers. Add a criss-cross layer of noodles. Top with the remaining Parmesan and ricotta cheeses. Add another criss-cross layer of noodles. Spoon the remaining combined mixture over the layers.

Top with the remaining mozzarella cheese and bake for 20-25 minutes or until golden and heated through. Let stand for 10 minutes for easier cutting. Serve.

Tortellini with Sun-Dried Tomato Sauce

YIELD: 6-8 SERVINGS
TIME: 45 MINUTES

4 tablespoons olive oil
½ cup chopped onions
2 cloves garlic, minced
One 28-ounce can plum tomatoes, chopped
½ cup sliced sun-dried tomatoes (see pages 275-276)
Salt and freshly ground black pepper to taste
24 ounces cheese-filled tortellini pasta

In a large skillet, heat the oil and sauté the onions and garlic until the onions are translucent. Add the plum tomatoes and cook for 15-20 minutes or until thick. Stir in the sun-dried tomatoes and cook for 8-10 minutes more. Add the salt and pepper.

Prepare the tortellini according to package directions. Drain and place in a large, warm serving bowl. Pour the tomato sauce over the pasta and serve immediately.

Ziti with Tuna Sauce

YIELD: 4 SERVINGS
TIME: 40 MINUTES

2 tablespoons olive oil
2 cloves garlic, minced
1 large red bell pepper, cored, seeded, and finely chopped
6 medium red tomatoes, chopped
One 6½-ounce can water-packed solid white tuna, drained
¼ cup chopped fresh oregano *or* 1 tablespoon dried oregano
½ teaspoon freshly ground black pepper
½ cup chopped fresh parsley
1 cup grated Parmesan cheese
1 pound ziti or penne pasta

In a large skillet, heat the oil and sauté the garlic for 10 seconds. Add the bell pepper and sauté for 2 minutes. Add the tomatoes. Reduce heat and simmer for 10 minutes.

Using a wooden spoon, crush the tuna into the tomato mixture. Stir in the oregano, black pepper, and ¼ cup parsley. Simmer for 10 minutes. In a small bowl, combine the cheese and the remaining parsley.

Prepare the ziti according to package directions. Drain and toss the pasta with the cheese mixture. Place in a large, warm serving bowl and top with the tuna mixture. Serve immediately.

Manicotti

YIELD: 6 SERVINGS
TIME: 1 HOUR

The filling for the manicotti can be made one day ahead. It also can be used to stuff cannelloni, ravioli, and jumbo shells.

4 cups tomato sauce
1 pound low-fat ricotta cheese
¾ cup grated Parmesan cheese
½ cup half-and-half
6 scallions, grated (include green tops)
¼ cup chopped fresh parsley
¼ teaspoon ground mace
⅛ teaspoon freshly ground black pepper
12 cooked manicotti shells
½ cup light cream (optional)
¼ cup grated Parmesan cheese

Preheat oven to 375° F. Pour ¼ cup tomato sauce in an oiled 9 by 13-inch baking dish to cover the bottom. Mix together the remaining ingredients, except the pasta shells, cream, and ¼ cup Parmesan cheese, until thoroughly combined.

Stuff the pasta shells with the combined mixture and place in a baking dish. Cover with the remaining tomato sauce and pour the cream over the top. Cover with aluminum foil and bake for 15 minutes.

Remove the aluminum foil and sprinkle with the remaining Parmesan cheese. Bake for 10 minutes more. Serve immediately.

Linguine with Red Clam Sauce

YIELD: 4 SERVINGS
TIME: 40 MINUTES

4 dozen littleneck clams, scrubbed
½ cup white wine
2 tablespoons olive oil
3 cloves garlic, minced
One 28-ounce can crushed tomatoes
1 teaspoon dried thyme
¼ teaspoon hot red pepper flakes
⅓ cup chopped fresh parsley
1 pound thin linguine pasta

In a large pot, steam the clams in the wine for 10 minutes, or until the shells open. Remove the clams from the shells and set aside. Reserve the clam broth.

In a medium-size skillet, heat the oil and sauté the garlic for 10 seconds. Add 1 cup of the reserved clam broth, the tomatoes, thyme, pepper flakes, and parsley. Simmer for 15 minutes.

Prepare the linguine according to package directions. Drain and place in a large, warm serving bowl. Stir the reserved clams into the clam broth mixture and heat through. Pour the clam mixture over the pasta and serve immediately.

French Bread Pizza

YIELD: 4-6 SERVINGS
TIME: 25 MINUTES

1 pound hot or sweet lean Italian bulk sausage
2 cups tomato sauce
2 cloves garlic, finely minced
1 teaspoon chopped fresh oregano
Salt and freshly ground black pepper to taste
1 loaf crusty, French bread, cut in half lengthwise
½ pound low-fat mozzarella cheese, shredded
½ cup grated Parmesan cheese

Preheat oven to 450° F. In a large skillet, sauté the sausage until lightly browned. Drain off the fat. Remove the sausage and set aside. Keep the sausage warm.

In a medium-size bowl, combine the tomato sauce, garlic, oregano, salt, and pepper. Divide this mixture between the two halves of bread and spread evenly over each half. Sprinkle the cheeses evenly over each half.

Sprinkle the reserved sausage over each half and place the halves on a baking sheet. Bake for 5-7 minutes, or until the cheese is bubbly. Serve hot.

Pizza with Potato Crust

YIELD: 4-6 SERVINGS
TIME: 45 MINUTES

●

4-5 medium potatoes
¼ cup olive oil
2 tablespoons toasted bread crumbs
¼ cup shredded low-fat mozzarella cheese
¼ cup grated Romano cheese
1 cup diced red tomatoes
1 teaspoon dried oregano

Boil the potatoes, unpeeled, until tender. Mash or put through a ricer. Stir in 3 tablespoons oil. Set aside.

Preheat oven to 450° F. Lightly oil a pizza pan. Sprinkle the bread crumbs on the pan. Spread the reserved potatoes on the pan, forming a thick edge with your fingers. Sprinkle the cheeses evenly on the potato crust. Add the tomatoes and oregano.

Drizzle the remaining oil over the pizza and bake for 20 minutes, or until the crust is golden on the edges. Serve hot.

Herbed Tomato Corn Bread

YIELD: 8 SERVINGS
TIME: 1 HOUR

1 cup unbleached all-purpose flour
⅔ cup whole wheat flour
3 teaspoons baking powder
½ teaspoon salt
2 tablespoons sugar or honey
¾ cup cornmeal
½ teaspoon dried basil
½ teaspoon dried thyme
1 teaspoon dried dill
1 egg
1½ cups tomato juice or puree
¼ cup vegetable oil

Preheat oven to 425° F. In a large bowl, sift the flours with the baking powder, salt, and sugar. (If you are using honey, mix it with the tomato juice.) Stir in the cornmeal and herbs.

In a medium-size bowl, beat the egg. Stir in the tomato juice and oil. Add this mixture all at once to the dry ingredients. Stir just enough to moisten the mixture.

Pour the batter into an oiled 8 by 8-inch baking pan and bake for 30 minutes or until golden on top. Cool on a wire rack.

Tomato Herb Bread

YIELD: 2 LOAVES
TIME: 4 HOURS

¼ cup warm water
1 tablespoon active dry yeast
2 tablespoons honey
2 cups warm tomato juice or puree
2 tablespoons vegetable oil
2 teaspoons salt
2 teaspoons dried basil
1 teaspoon dried marjoram
4 cups unbleached all-purpose flour
2 cups whole wheat flour
1 egg, beaten

In a large bowl, combine the water, yeast, and honey. Stir well and set aside for 10 minutes until foamy.

Add the tomato juice, oil, salt, and herbs. Stir in 3 cups unbleached flour, 1 cup at a time, and beat until smooth and elastic. Mix in the remaining unbleached flour and beat well. Sprinkle a large surface with ½ cup whole wheat flour and turn the dough out onto the surface. Knead in the remaining whole wheat flour. If the dough is too sticky, add unbleached flour until the dough is a firm, smooth consistency. Knead the dough for 10 minutes.

Oil a large bowl and place the dough in the bowl. Let the bread rise for 1 hour 30 minutes in a warm place.

Punch the dough down and shape it into two loaves. Put in oiled loaf pans and let rise for 45 minutes. Preheat oven to 375° F. Brush the tops of the loaves with the egg. Bake for 25-30 minutes. Cool on wire racks.

Spicy Tomato Nut Cake

YIELD: 12 SERVINGS
TIME: 1 HOUR 30 MINUTES

●

½ cup butter or soft margarine
1½ cups granulated sugar
1 cup firmly packed brown sugar
3 cups unbleached all-purpose flour
1 cup whole wheat pastry flour
2½ teaspoons baking soda
2 teaspoons ground cinnamon
1½ teaspoons salt
1 teaspoon ground nutmeg
½ teaspoon ground allspice
2½ cups tomato juice or puree
2 teaspoons pure vanilla extract
1 cup chopped walnuts

Preheat oven to 350° F. In a large bowl, cream together the butter and sugars. In another large bowl, mix together all the dry ingredients and add them separately with the tomato juice to the creamed mixture. Stir in the vanilla extract and walnuts.

Pour the batter into an oiled bundt pan or ring-shaped cake pan. Bake for 1 hour 10 minutes, or until a tester inserted in the center comes out clean. Allow to cool for 10 minutes on a wire rack. Unmold onto a serving dish.

Red Tomato Catsup

YIELD: 5 HALF-PINT JARS
TIME: 2 HOURS

Italian plum tomatoes make the best catsup because they have less water than other varieties.

6 pounds red plum tomatoes, cored, peeled, and coarsely chopped
1 large onion, chopped
1 medium red bell pepper, cored, seeded, and diced
2 teaspoons celery seeds
1½ teaspoons allspice berries
1 teaspoon mustard seeds
2 cinnamon sticks
½ cup honey
1 tablespoon salt
1¼ cups cider vinegar

In a large stainless steel or enameled pot, combine the vegetables. Cook, uncovered, on medium heat for 30 minutes, stirring frequently. Puree in a blender or food processor and return the mixture to the pot. Tie the celery seeds, allspice berries, mustard seeds, and cinnamon sticks in a muslin bag and add to the pot. Add the honey, salt, and vinegar. Simmer for 20-30 minutes or until thick, stirring occasionally. Remove the spice bag.

Fill hot, sterilized half-pint jars with the tomato mixture, leaving a ½-inch headspace. Seal and process in a boiling water bath for 10 minutes. (See pages 276-277.)

Old-Time Hot Dog Relish

YIELD: 12 HALF-PINT JARS
TIME: 3 HOURS 20 MINUTES

5 pounds red tomatoes, cored, peeled, and finely chopped
2 medium red bell peppers, cored, seeded, and finely chopped
3 large onions, finely chopped
9 medium peaches, peeled and finely chopped
1½ cups cider vinegar
1½ cups honey
1 tablespoon pickling salt
4 tablespoons mixed pickling spices in a muslin bag

In a large stainless steel or enameled pot, combine the vegetables and fruit. Add the vinegar, honey, salt, and pickling spices. Cook, uncovered, on medium heat for 2 hours or until thick, stirring occasionally. Remove the spice bag.

Fill hot, sterilized half-pint jars with the tomato mixture, leaving a ½-inch headspace. Seal and process in a boiling water bath for 10 minutes. (See pages 276-277.)

Grandma's Old-Fashioned Chile Relish

YIELD: 4-5 PINTS
TIME: 3 HOURS 25 MINUTES

6 pounds red tomatoes, cored, peeled, and chopped
2 medium green bell peppers, cored, seeded, and chopped
2 medium red bell peppers, cored, seeded, and chopped
1 cup chopped celery with leaves
4 cups coarsely chopped onions
1 clove garlic, minced
2 bay leaves
1 cup firmly packed dark brown sugar
1½ cups cider vinegar
1 teaspoon ground cinnamon
½ teaspoon ground cloves
½ teaspoon ground ginger
1 teaspoon ground mustard
Dash cayenne powder
¼ teaspoon freshly ground black pepper
Salt to taste

In a large stainless steel or enameled pot, combine the tomatoes, bell peppers, celery, onions, garlic, bay leaves, brown sugar, and vinegar. Simmer for 1 hour, stirring occasionally.

Stir in the cinnamon, cloves, ginger, mustard, and cayenne powder. Continue to simmer for 2 hours, stirring occasionally. Add the black pepper and salt. Remove the bay leaves. Cool slightly.

Fill hot, sterilized pint jars with the tomato mixture, leaving a ½-inch headspace. Seal and process in a boiling water bath for 10 minutes. (See pages 276-277.)

Kiwifruit & Tomato Relish

YIELD: 3 HALF-PINT JARS
TIME: 1 HOUR

●

3 pounds red tomatoes, cored, peeled, and coarsely chopped
8 kiwifruit, peeled and coarsely chopped
2 large onions, chopped
1 medium green bell pepper, cored, seeded, and chopped
1 medium yellow bell pepper, cored, seeded, and chopped
1½ cups honey
2 cups white vinegar

In a large stainless steel or enameled pot, combine all the ingredients. Simmer for 30 minutes or until very thick, stirring occasionally.

Fill hot, sterilized half-pint jars with the tomato mixture, leaving a ½-inch headspace. Seal and process in a boiling water bath for 10 minutes. (See pages 276-277.)

Fruit & Tomato Chutney

YIELD: 11 HALF-PINT JARS
TIME: 2 HOURS

4 pounds red tomatoes, cored, peeled, and chopped
5 large green sour apples, cored, peeled, and chopped
1 large onion, diced
2 cloves garlic, minced
1½ cups raisins
1 cup diced dried apricots
1 cup cider vinegar
2 teaspoons salt
1 teaspoon ground cinnamon
Dash cayenne powder
⅓ cup finely diced candied ginger

In a stainless steel or enameled pot, combine all the ingredients. Cook, uncovered, on medium heat for 1 hour 30 minutes or until very thick, stirring occasionally.

Fill hot, sterilized half-pint jars with the tomato mixture, leaving a ½-inch headspace. Seal and process in a boiling water bath for 10 minutes. (See pages 276-277.)

Lemon Tomato Jelly

YIELD: 4 HALF-PINT JARS
TIME: 30 MINUTES

●

2 cups tomato juice

½ cup fresh lemon juice, strained

2 cups sugar

2 cinnamon sticks

2 cups honey

3 ounces liquid pectin

In a large stainless steel or enameled pot, combine the tomato juice, lemon juice, sugar, cinnamon sticks, and honey. Bring to a rapid boil. Remove from heat and let stand for 15 minutes. Remove the cinnamon sticks.

Add the pectin and return the mixture to a rapid boil for 1 minute. Remove from heat and skim off any froth.

Fill hot, sterilized half-pint jars with the tomato mixture, leaving a ¼-inch headspace. Seal according to manufacturer's directions.

Tomato Herb Jelly

YIELD: 4 HALF-PINT JARS
TIME: 45 MINUTES

¼ cup chopped fresh sage *or* ¼ cup crushed fresh marjoram
¼ cup crushed fresh thyme
1 cup water
1 cup tomato juice
Dash Tabasco sauce
½ cup fresh lemon juice, strained
2 cups honey
2 cups sugar
6 ounces liquid pectin

In a small saucepan, combine the herbs with the water. Simmer gently for 5 minutes. Remove from heat and let stand for 30 minutes.

In a large stainless steel or enameled pot, combine the tomato juice, Tabasco sauce, lemon juice, honey, and sugar. Strain the herbs. Add the herb water and 2 teaspoons of the cooked herbs to the tomato mixture. Bring to a rapid boil. Add the pectin and boil rapidly for 1 minute. Remove from heat and skim off any froth.

Fill hot, sterilized half-pint jars with the tomato mixture, leaving a ¼-inch headspace. Seal according to manufacturer's directions.

Tomato & Pear Marmalade

YIELD: 4 PINTS
TIME: 1 HOUR

1 medium orange
2 medium lemons
½ cup water
3 pounds red tomatoes, cored, peeled, and chopped
2 pounds pears, cored, peeled, and thinly sliced
5 cups sugar
2 tablespoons candied ginger

Squeeze the orange and lemons; strain and reserve the juice. Peel the skin off the orange and lemons in thin strips, removing as much of the white membrane as possible. Cut the citrus strips into thinner strips.

In a small saucepan, boil the water and add the citrus peel. Reduce heat and simmer for 15 minutes. Drain and set aside.

In a large stainless steel or enameled pot, combine the reserved lemon juice, reserved citrus peel, tomatoes, pears, sugar, and ginger. Bring to a boil. Reduce heat and simmer for 2 hours or until thick, stirring occasionally.

Fill hot, sterilized pint jars with the tomato mixture, leaving a ¼-inch headspace. Seal according to manufacturer's directions.

3

Green Tomato Delights

Bacon Cheese Ball

YIELD: 8-10 SERVINGS
TIME: 20 MINUTES PLUS CHILLING TIME

●

1 pound low-fat cream cheese
½ pound lean bacon, browned and crumbled
4 scallions, finely diced
1 medium green tomato, finely chopped
1 cup finely chopped walnuts

In a small bowl, mix all the ingredients, except the nuts, and form into a ball. Cover with the walnuts. Chill for at least 1 hour before serving. Serve.

Green Tomato Nacho Bean Dip

YIELD: 8 SERVINGS
TIME: 30 MINUTES

●

2 tablespoons vegetable oil
1 medium onion, diced
2 medium green tomatoes, diced
2 cups cooked red kidney beans
1½ cups *Red Taco Sauce* (see page 118)
Salt and freshly ground black pepper to taste
1½ cups shredded low-fat cheddar cheese
Corn chips

In a large skillet, heat the oil and sauté the onion until translucent. Add the tomatoes and cook for 5 minutes. Add the beans, 1 cup *Red Taco Sauce*, salt, and pepper. Continue cooking for 15 minutes. Mash some of the beans with the back of a spoon to make the mixture look pasty.

Put the mixture into a shallow baking dish. Sprinkle the cheese and remaining *Red Taco Sauce* on top. Broil for 5 minutes, or until the cheese is bubbly. Serve with the corn chips.

Spiced Carrot Soup

YIELD: 6 SERVINGS
TIME: 45 MINUTES

1 pound carrots, diced
4 large green tomatoes, diced
1 medium onion, diced
7 cups chicken or vegetable broth
3 teaspoons ground ginger
1 teaspoon ground nutmeg
1 cup half-and-half
1 tablespoon honey
Salt and freshly ground black pepper to taste

In a large pot, combine the vegetables and chicken broth. Simmer for 15 minutes, or until the vegetables are tender. Cool slightly.

In a blender or food processor, blend the mixture until smooth. Return the mixture to the pot and add the remaining ingredients. Reheat and serve.

Sweet Potato Soup

YIELD: 8 SERVINGS
TIME: 1 HOUR 30 MINUTES

5 medium sweet potatoes
5 medium green tomatoes, diced
¼ cup water
4 cups low-fat milk
2 tablespoons vegetable oil
1 large onion, diced
2 cups diced zucchini
3 cloves garlic, minced
1½ cups peas, fresh or frozen
1 tablespoon honey
1 pound low-fat cheddar cheese, shredded
3 tablespoons tamari or salt to taste

Cut the potatoes into pieces, but do not peel. In a large pot with enough water to cover, boil the potatoes until soft. Drain and peel.

In a medium-size saucepan, cook the tomatoes in the water until soft. Puree the potatoes and tomatoes together in a blender or food processor, adding as much milk as necessary to achieve a soup consistency. Return the potato mixture to the saucepan.

In a small saucepan, heat the oil and sauté the onion and zucchini until tender crisp. Add to the large saucepan. Add the remaining ingredients. Reheat the soup on low heat and serve.

Green Tomato Borscht

YIELD: 6 SERVINGS
TIME: 2 HOURS

2 tablespoons vegetable oil
5 medium green tomatoes, finely chopped
1 medium onion, finely diced
3 cups cooked diced beets
1 pound lean beef, cooked and diced
6 cups beef broth
4 tablespoons honey
3 tablespoons fresh lemon juice
Salt and freshly ground black pepper to taste
½ pound lean bacon, cooked and diced (optional)
½ cup low-fat sour cream, for garnish

In a large pot, heat the oil and sauté the tomatoes, onion, beets, and beef for 10 minutes. Add the remaining ingredients, except the sour cream, and simmer for 1 hour 30 minutes. Garnish with the sour cream and serve.

Tomato Mushroom Soup

YIELD: 8 SERVINGS
TIME: 1 HOUR 15 MINUTES

2 tablespoons vegetable oil
2 large onions, diced
1½ pounds fresh mushrooms, sliced
2 medium potatoes, diced
2 cups finely diced green tomatoes
6 cups water
2 teaspoons dried dill
2 tablespoons Hungarian paprika
¼ cup tamari or soy sauce
3 tablespoons butter or soft margarine
3 tablespoons unbleached all-purpose flour
2 cups low-fat milk
Salt and freshly ground black pepper to taste
¼ cup fresh lemon juice
1 cup low-fat sour cream

In a large pot, heat the oil and sauté the onions and mushrooms for 5 minutes. Add the potatoes and tomatoes and cook for 5 minutes. Add the water, dill, paprika, and tamari. Cover and cook for 20 minutes.

In a small saucepan, melt the butter and add the flour, stirring constantly to prevent lumps. Slowly add the milk and continue stirring to make a thick white sauce. Add some of the mixture from the pot to the white sauce and mix well. Return the white sauce to the pot. Cover and simmer for 10 minutes. Just before serving, add the salt, pepper, lemon juice, and sour cream. Stir well and serve.

Carrot Salad

YIELD: 4 SERVINGS
TIME: 20 MINUTES

1 cup shredded carrots
2 medium green tomatoes, peeled and diced
1 cup diced celery
Lettuce
Creamy French Dressing (see page 198)

In a medium-size bowl, combine the carrots, tomatoes, and celery. Arrange on servings of crisp lettuce and top with the *Creamy French Dressing*. Serve.

Cabbage & Apple Salad

YIELD: 6-8 SERVINGS
TIME: 40 MINUTES

1 medium head green cabbage
1 cup diced celery
2 cups unpeeled and diced red apples
1 medium green bell pepper, cored, seeded, and diced
½ cup chopped walnuts or pecans
2 medium green tomatoes, chopped
½ cup *Sweet & Sour Dressing* (see page 196)
Lettuce
Unpeeled red apple slices, for garnish

Remove the coarse outer leaves from the cabbage. Cut an even slice off the top. Invert the cabbage and remove the core in one piece. Using a sharp knife, remove most of the inner portion of the cabbage from the cored end, leaving a solid shell which stands upright. Trim the top evenly.

From the inner portion, prepare 2 cups shredded cabbage. Combine the shredded cabbage with the celery, apples, green pepper, walnuts, and tomatoes. Add the *Sweet & Sour Dressing* and toss lightly. Place the cabbage mixture into the cabbage shell.

Line a serving platter with crisp lettuce, place the cabbage shell in the center, and garnish with the apple slices. Serve.

Green Mountain Coleslaw

YIELD: 8-10 SERVINGS
TIME: 25 MINUTES PLUS STANDING TIME

1 large head green cabbage, shredded
3 large carrots, grated
3 medium green tomatoes, finely diced
3 medium apples, cored and diced
½ cup chopped walnuts
¾ cup raisins
1½ cups low-calorie mayonnaise
¼ cup pure maple syrup
¾ teaspoon ground nutmeg

In a large bowl, combine the cabbage, carrots, tomatoes, apples, walnuts, and raisins.

In a small bowl, whisk together the remaining ingredients and pour over the salad. Mix well and let the salad sit for 1 hour before serving. Serve.

Carrot Confetti in Pineapple Boats

YIELD: 6-8 SERVINGS
TIME: 30 MINUTES

3 cups grated carrots
2 medium green tomatoes, finely chopped
½ cup raisins
½ cup chopped walnuts
1 fresh pineapple
⅓ cup honey or pure maple syrup
½ cup fresh lemon juice
¼ cup chopped fresh parsley, for garnish

In a large bowl, mix together the carrots, tomatoes, raisins, and walnuts.

Cut the pineapple in half horizontally, leaving the green top attached. Core the pineapple and scoop out the pulp, leaving "boats" of the pineapple shells. Chop the pulp and add to the carrot mixture.

In a small bowl, mix the honey and lemon juice. Combine the honey mixture with the carrot mixture. Pile the carrot salad into the empty pineapple shells. Garnish with the parsley and serve.

Fruit Salad

YIELD: 6 SERVINGS
TIME: 20 MINUTES

1 medium orange
2 medium green tomatoes, chopped
2 teaspoons sugar
3 medium fresh peaches *or* 6 canned peach halves, chopped
¼ cup finely diced celery
¼ cup finely diced apples
Low-calorie mayonnaise
Lettuce
6 fresh Bing cherries

Peel the orange and chop the pulp. Combine the orange pulp with the tomatoes and sugar. Set aside for 5 minutes.

Combine the orange mixture with the peaches, celery, and apples. Moisten the mixture with the mayonnaise. Serve on crisp lettuce garnished with the cherries.

Green Goddess Dressing

YIELD: 1¾ CUPS
TIME: 10 MINUTES

1 cup finely chopped green tomatoes
1 tablespoon chopped fresh tarragon *or* 2 teaspoons dried tarragon
¼ cup finely diced fresh chives
½ cup finely chopped fresh parsley
2 cloves garlic, minced
2 tablespoons tarragon vinegar
1½ cups low-calorie mayonnaise
Salt and freshly ground black pepper to taste

In a blender or food processor, combine the tomatoes, herbs, and garlic and blend well. Add the vinegar, mayonnaise, salt, and pepper. Mix lightly. The dressing will keep for 1-2 weeks in the refrigerator.

Sweet & Sour Dressing

YIELD: 3 CUPS
TIME: 10 MINUTES

2 cups vegetable oil
½ cup red wine vinegar
½ teaspoon salt
Freshly ground black pepper to taste
3 small green tomatoes, chopped
1 heaping tablespoon Dijon mustard
2 tablespoons honey, or to taste

In a blender or food processor, combine all the ingredients and blend until smooth. The dressing will keep for 1-2 weeks in the refrigerator.

Thousand Island Dressing

YIELD: 2 CUPS
TIME: 10 MINUTES

2 medium green tomatoes
1 cup low-calorie mayonnaise
1 tablespoon chopped green bell pepper
1 tablespoon chopped red bell pepper
¼ teaspoon ground paprika
2 tablespoons chopped green olives

Peel the tomatoes. Scoop out the seeds and pulp and discard. Finely chop the outer shells.

In a small bowl, combine the tomatoes with the remaining ingredients and mix well. The dressing will keep for 1-2 weeks in the refrigerator.

Creamy French Dressing

YIELD: 2 CUPS
TIME: 10 MINUTES

2 medium green tomatoes
4 tablespoons fresh lemon juice or white wine vinegar
4 tablespoons catsup
¼ teaspoon ground paprika
¼ teaspoon salt
⅛ teaspoon garlic powder
1 tablespoon honey
Dash cayenne powder
½ cup vegetable oil

Peel the tomatoes. Scoop out the seeds and pulp and discard. Coarsely chop the outer shells and put in a blender or food processor. Add the lemon juice, catsup, paprika, salt, garlic powder, honey, and cayenne powder. Blend until smooth.

Gradually add the oil, one teaspoon at a time, on low speed. The dressing will keep for 1-2 weeks in the refrigerator.

Fried Green Tomatoes

YIELD: VARIABLE
TIME: 20 MINUTES

●

Fried green tomatoes are one of the few dishes that are "standard" for green tomatoes. You can make your green tomatoes very "unstandard" by varying the breading or seasoning.

Eggs and milk
1 medium green tomato per person
2 tablespoons vegetable oil

BREADINGS
(approximately ½ cup per tomato):
Cornmeal, bread crumbs, wheat germ, or unbleached all-purpose flour

SEASONINGS
(½ teaspoon per tomato):
Grated Parmesan cheese, salt and freshly ground black pepper, Italian herbs, caraway seeds, curry powder, sesame seeds, or chile powder

OILS
(2 tablespoons per tomato):
Vegetable oil, olive oil, butter, or soft margarine

Beat the eggs and combine with the milk (approximately 2 tablespoons milk per egg). Combine the breading with the seasoning of your choice.

Slice the tomatoes into ½-inch slices. Dip the tomatoes into the egg mixture. Cover with the seasoned breading. In a large skillet, heat the oil and fry the tomatoes until crispy golden brown on both sides. Serve immediately.

Stewed Green Tomatoes

YIELD: 6-8 SERVINGS
TIME: 25 MINUTES

2 tablespoons vegetable oil
3 medium onions, thinly sliced
6 large green tomatoes, cut into ¼-inch slices
½ cup water
2 tablespoons butter or soft margarine
1 tablespoon sugar
½ teaspoon salt

In a large skillet, heat the oil and sauté the onions until translucent. Add the tomatoes and sauté for 3 minutes, stirring occasionally. Add the water, cover, and simmer for 10 minutes, or until the tomatoes are soft.

Add the butter, sugar, and salt. Cook for 3 minutes more and serve.

Baked Green Tomatoes

YIELD: 6 SERVINGS
TIME: 45 MINUTES

6 large green tomatoes
Salt to taste
8 eggs
½ teaspoon salt
¼ teaspoon dried basil
2 tablespoons vegetable oil
1 cup shredded low-fat cheddar cheese
1 cup bread cubes
¼ cup grated Parmesan cheese

Preheat oven to 350° F. Cut the tops off the tomatoes. Remove the seeds and pulp, reserving enough pulp to make 1 cup. Discard remaining pulp. Salt the insides of the tomato shells and set aside.

In a small bowl, slightly beat the eggs with a fork. Add the salt and basil. In a large skillet, heat the oil and add the egg mixture. Cook on low heat, stirring frequently, until the eggs are set, but still slightly moist.

Combine the egg mixture with the cheddar cheese, bread cubes, and the reserved 1 cup tomato pulp. Spoon the tomato mixture into the tomato shells and place the shells in a shallow baking dish. Top with the Parmesan cheese and bake for 15 minutes.

Green tomato shells also may be filled with any of the following:

Macaroni and cheese
Cooked succotash
Bread stuffing with cooked chopped meat or sautéed mushrooms
Spanish Rice (see page 257)

Bake in a 350° F. oven for 20 minutes. Serve hot.

Log Cabin Potatoes

YIELD: 8 SERVINGS
TIME: 1 HOUR 30 MINUTES

8 medium unpeeled potatoes, thinly sliced
3 large green tomatoes, thinly sliced
1 medium onion, diced
1 cup unbleached all-purpose flour
1 pound low-fat cheddar cheese, grated
¼ pound lean bacon, cooked and crumbled
Salt and freshly ground black pepper to taste
½ cup low-fat milk

Preheat oven to 350° F. Oil a large baking dish. Alternate layers of the potatoes and tomatoes. Sprinkle on a little of the onion, flour, cheese, bacon, salt, and pepper between layers. Continue layering until the dish is full, ending with a layer of cheese.

Pour the milk over the top and bake for 1 hour, or until the potatoes are cooked and bubbly brown on top. Serve.

Vermont Sweet Potatoes

YIELD: 8 SERVINGS
TIME: 1 HOUR

6 medium sweet potatoes, cooked and thinly sliced
5 medium green tomatoes, sliced
4 tablespoons butter or soft margarine
½ cup pure maple syrup
1 cup shredded coconut

Preheat oven to 350° F. Oil a large baking dish. Alternate layers of the potatoes and tomatoes. Continue layering until the dish is full.

In a small saucepan, melt the butter and add the maple syrup. Pour the butter mixture over the potatoes. Sprinkle the coconut on top. Bake, uncovered, for 30 minutes or until bubbly. Serve.

Yellow Confetti Rice

YIELD: 6 SERVINGS
TIME: 50 MINUTES

4 cups water
½ teaspoon salt
2 cups uncooked brown rice
⅛ teaspoon saffron *or* ½ teaspoon turmeric
1 small onion, diced
1 medium green tomato, diced
½ cup raisins
½ cup chopped walnuts

In a medium-size saucepan, bring the water to a boil. Add the salt, rice, saffron, and onion. Cover the saucepan. Reduce heat and simmer for 30 minutes.

Add the tomato to the saucepan, but do not stir. Continue cooking for 15 minutes more. The rice should be tender and the water absorbed. Remove from heat and stir in the raisins and nuts, using a fork to fluff up the rice. Serve hot.

Jubilee Carrots

YIELD: 8 SERVINGS
TIME: 10 MINUTES

●

1 pound carrots, sliced
½ cup water
2 medium green tomatoes, diced
2 tablespoons butter or soft margarine
¼ cup packed brown sugar
1 tablespoon Dijon mustard
Salt and freshly ground black pepper to taste

In a medium-size saucepan, simmer the carrots in the water for 5 minutes, uncovered. Add the tomatoes and cook for 5 minutes. Add the remaining ingredients and cook for 3 minutes more. Serve hot.

Spaghetti Squash Supreme

YIELD: 8 SERVINGS
TIME: 1 HOUR 30 MINUTES

1 medium spaghetti squash
4 tablespoons olive oil
1 medium eggplant, peeled and cut into ½-inch cubes
3 medium green tomatoes, cut into ½-inch cubes
3 cloves garlic, minced
½ cup chopped fresh parsley
Salt and freshly ground black pepper to taste
2 tablespoons butter or soft margarine
½ pound fresh mushrooms, sliced
1 cup grated low-fat cheddar cheese

Preheat oven to 400° F. Pierce the skin of the spaghetti squash in several places with a fork. Bake for 45 minutes, or until the squash feels soft when you press.

In a large skillet, heat the oil and sauté the eggplant for 5 minutes. Add the tomatoes and garlic and cook for 10 minutes. Add the parsley, salt, and pepper. Set aside.

Cut the cooked squash in half lengthwise and scoop out the seeds. Use a fork to remove all the pulp from the squash. Set aside the pulp and discard the skin. In a small skillet, melt the butter and sauté the mushrooms until tender. Drain off the liquid, add the reserved squash pulp, and heat. Reheat the eggplant mixture. Place the squash mixture in a casserole dish. Sprinkle with the cheese. Pour the eggplant mixture on top. Serve immediately.

Mock-Apple Slices

YIELD: 6 SERVINGS
TIME: 50 MINUTES

16 small green tomatoes
1 lemon slice
¾ cup sugar
½ cup water
1 tablespoon finely grated fresh gingerroot*
¼ teaspoon salt

Preheat oven to 350° F. Peel and core the tomatoes. Remove the seeds and pulp and discard. Cut the fleshy outer shell into strips and spread in an oiled baking dish.

In a small bowl, combine the remaining ingredients and pour over the tomato strips. Cover and bake for 20 minutes. Uncover and bake for 20 minutes more. Serve.

*If desired, ½ teaspoon ground cinnamon and ¼ teaspoon ground ginger may be substituted for the fresh gingerroot.

Pasta Charlotte

YIELD: 6-8 SERVINGS
TIME: 1 HOUR

4 cups chopped green tomatoes
½ cup white wine
2 tablespoons butter or soft margarine
1 large onion, diced
1 cup half-and-half
¼ cup finely chopped fresh basil
1 teaspoon honey
Salt and freshly ground black pepper to taste
2 pounds rotini pasta
Grated Parmesan cheese, for garnish
1 cup sliced black olives, for garnish

In a large saucepan, combine the tomatoes and wine. Cook, uncovered, for 45 minutes, stirring occasionally. In a blender or food processor, puree the mixture and set aside.

In a large saucepan, melt the butter and sauté the onion. Add the reserved tomato puree, half-and-half, basil, honey, salt, and pepper. Keep the sauce warm.

Prepare the rotini according to package directions. Drain and place the pasta in a large, warm serving bowl. Pour the sauce over the top and sprinkle with the cheese and black olives. Serve immediately.

Old-Fashioned Chicken Pot Pie

YIELD: 6 SERVINGS
TIME: 1 HOUR 30 MINUTES

FILLING:

4 tablespoons butter or soft margarine
4 large green tomatoes, chopped
3 large carrots, diced
1 large onion, diced
4 stalks celery, diced
4 cups cooked diced chicken
½ cup butter or soft margarine
½ cup unbleached all-purpose flour
3 cups low-fat milk
¼ cup chopped fresh basil *or* 2 teaspoons dried basil
Salt and freshly ground black pepper to taste

BISCUIT DOUGH:

2 cups unbleached all-purpose flour
½ teaspoon salt
4 teaspoons baking powder
½ teaspoon cream of tartar
⅓ cup low-fat milk
1 cup whipped topping

Preheat oven to 350° F. In a large skillet, melt the 4 tablespoons butter and sauté the vegetables for 10 minutes. In a large bowl, combine the vegetables and the chicken.

In the same skillet, melt the ½ cup butter and add the ½ cup flour, stirring constantly to prevent lumps. Slowly stir in the 3 cups milk to make a thick white sauce. Add the white sauce and the basil to the chicken mixture. Add the salt and pepper. Put the chicken mixture into an oiled baking dish.

BISCUIT DOUGH: Sift together the 2 cups flour, salt, baking powder, and cream of tartar. Fold the flour mixture and the ⅓ cup milk in with the whipped topping, stirring just enough to mix. Drop the biscuit dough by spoonsful onto the chicken mixture to cover the top. Bake for 25 minutes, or until the biscuits begin to brown. Serve.

Chicken Dijon with Green Tomatoes

YIELD: 6 SERVINGS
TIME: 1 HOUR 30 MINUTES

This dish can be made early in the day, refrigerated, and reheated for 45 minutes before serving.

2 tablespoons vegetable oil
6 pieces chicken, skinned
½ cup butter or soft margarine
¾ cup unbleached all-purpose flour
1½ cups low-fat milk
¾ cup white wine
4 tablespoons Dijon mustard
1 tablespoon vegetable oil
5 medium green tomatoes, finely diced
Salt and freshly ground black pepper to taste
Cooked rice or noodles

Preheat oven to 400° F. In a large skillet, heat the 2 tablespoons oil and brown the chicken on both sides. Remove the chicken and place in a baking dish.

In a medium-size skillet, melt the butter. Mix the flour into the butter. Slowly add the milk, a little at a time, stirring constantly to prevent any lumps. Add the wine and mustard. Cook the mustard sauce for 10 minutes on low heat.

In a medium-size saucepan, heat the 1 tablespoon oil and sauté the tomatoes for 10 minutes. Add the tomatoes to the mustard sauce. Add the salt and pepper. Pour the sauce on top of the chicken and bake for 30-45 minutes. Serve over the rice or noodles.

Green Tomato Tarragon Chicken

YIELD: 6 SERVINGS
TIME: 1 HOUR 30 MINUTES

2 tablespoons vegetable oil
6 pieces chicken, skinned
4 cups diced green tomatoes
½ cup water
1 tablespoon honey
1 cup half-and-half
1 tablespoon dried tarragon
Salt and freshly ground black pepper to taste
Cooked rice or noodles
Grated Parmesan cheese, for garnish

Preheat oven to 350° F. In a large skillet, heat the oil and brown the chicken on both sides. Remove the chicken and place in a baking dish.

In a medium-size saucepan, combine the tomatoes, water, and honey and cook for 30 minutes, or until the tomatoes are soft. In a blender or food processor, puree the tomatoes with the cooking liquid.

Add the half-and-half, tarragon, salt, and pepper. Pour this mixture over the chicken and bake for 45-60 minutes. Serve over the rice or noodles and garnish with the cheese.

Curried Chicken

YIELD: 6 SERVINGS
TIME: 45 MINUTES

●

3 chicken breasts, boned, skinned, and cut into ½-inch cubes
1½ cups unbleached all-purpose flour
¼ cup vegetable oil
2 tablespoons vegetable oil
5 large green tomatoes, diced
1 large onion, sliced
½ cup apple cider
2 tablespoons curry powder
½ teaspoon ground cumin
½ teaspoon ground coriander
Dash cayenne powder
1 cup half-and-half
Salt to taste
Cooked rice

Dredge the chicken with the flour. In a large skillet, heat the ¼ cup oil and brown the chicken for 10 minutes. Remove the chicken from the skillet. Drain off the fat. Add the 2 tablespoons oil to the skillet and sauté the vegetables for 10 minutes.

Mix together the cider, curry powder, cumin, coriander, and cayenne powder, and add to the vegetables. Add the reserved chicken, half-and-half, and salt. Simmer for 10 minutes to let the flavors mingle. Serve over the rice.

Stroganoff Stew

YIELD: 6 SERVINGS
TIME: 2 HOURS

½ pound lean bacon, diced
¾ cup unbleached all-purpose flour
1 teaspoon salt
½ teaspoon freshly ground black pepper
2 teaspoons mixed Italian herbs*
1½ pounds lean stew beef
2 tablespoons vegetable oil
5 medium green tomatoes, finely chopped
1 medium onion, chopped
3 cups water
1 pound fresh mushrooms, sliced
2 cups low-fat sour cream
3 tablespoons cornstarch mixed with 3 tablespoons water (optional)
¼ cup tamari
¼ cup chopped fresh basil *or* 2 tablespoons dried basil
Cooked noodles

In a large saucepan, cook the bacon. Remove the bacon pieces and set aside. Drain off the fat.

In a medium-size bowl, mix together the flour, salt, pepper, and herbs. Dredge the beef in the flour mixture. In the saucepan, sauté the meat in the oil until browned. Add the tomatoes, onion, water, and any remaining flour. Cover the saucepan and simmer for 1 hour 30 minutes.

Add the mushrooms and sour cream. (For a thicker gravy, make a paste by combining the cornstarch with the water and add to the sour cream, before adding the sour cream to the saucepan.) Cook on low heat for 15 minutes and add the tamari and basil. Serve over the noodles.

* Make your own mix of Italian herbs by combining equal portions of basil, oregano, thyme, marjoram, and rosemary.

. . . .

Creamy Egg & Tomato Casserole

YIELD: 4-6 SERVINGS
TIME: 50 MINUTES

6 hard-cooked eggs, sliced
1½ cups chopped green tomatoes
5 tablespoons butter or soft margarine
¾ cup soft bread crumbs
3 tablespoons unbleached all-purpose flour
1½ cups low-fat milk

Preheat oven to 350° F. In a shallow baking dish, alternate layers of the egg slices and tomatoes. Set aside.

In a small saucepan, melt 2 tablespoons butter and add the bread crumbs. Stir well and set aside.

In a medium-size saucepan, melt the remaining butter and stir in the flour. Gradually add the milk and cook on low heat, stirring constantly until thick. Pour the milk mixture over the reserved egg and tomato layers and top with the reserved bread crumbs. Bake for 35-40 minutes. Serve immediately.

Spinach Loaf with Green Tomato Sauce

YIELD: 6 SERVINGS
TIME: 45 MINUTES

2 eggs, well beaten
1 cup cooked chopped spinach
2½ cups chopped green tomatoes
1 cup shredded low-fat cheddar cheese
1 cup soft bread crumbs
Salt and freshly ground black pepper to taste
2 tablespoons vegetable oil
1 tablespoon minced onions
1 tablespoon chopped green bell peppers
2 tablespoons unbleached all-purpose flour

Preheat oven to 350° F. In a small bowl, combine the eggs, spinach, 1 cup tomatoes, cheese, bread crumbs, salt, and pepper. Pour the egg mixture into an oiled loaf pan and bake for 30 minutes.

SAUCE: In a medium-size skillet, heat the oil and sauté the onions and green peppers. Add the remaining tomatoes and stir-fry for 3-5 minutes, or until the tomatoes are cooked. Stir in the flour and cook until thick. Pour the sauce over the hot *Spinach Loaf*. Serve.

Sesame Green Tomato Quiche

YIELD: 8 SERVINGS
TIME: 1 HOUR 45 MINUTES

CRUST:

1 cup unbleached all-purpose flour
¼ teaspoon salt
¼ cup sesame seeds
⅓ cup vegetable shortening
2-4 tablespoons water

FILLING:

2 tablespoons vegetable oil
1 medium onion, diced
2 medium green tomatoes, finely diced
2 cups sliced fresh mushrooms
1½ cups cooked diced ham (optional)
4 eggs
2 cups half-and-half
Dash ground nutmeg
½ teaspoon salt
Dash freshly ground black pepper
½ pound Swiss cheese, grated
2 tablespoons sesame seeds

In a large bowl, combine the flour, salt, and ¼ cup sesame seeds. Cut the shortening into the flour and blend with a fork until the mixture resembles small peas. Add the water and mix until the dough forms a ball. Refrigerate the dough for 30 minutes.

In a medium-size saucepan, heat the oil and sauté the onion for 5 minutes. Add the tomatoes and mushrooms and cook for 3 minutes.

Cool slightly.

Preheat oven to 350° F. Roll out the crust on a lightly floured surface. Fit it into a 10-inch pie pan and flute the edges. Spread the vegetables over the bottom crust and sprinkle the ham over the vegetables.

In a large bowl, beat together the eggs, half-and-half, nutmeg, salt, and pepper. Pour the egg mixture into the crust. Sprinkle the cheese evenly over the quiche and top with the 2 tablespoons sesame seeds. Bake for 1 hour or until golden brown on top. Serve hot.

Fruited Tea Bread

YIELD: 12 SERVINGS
TIME: 1 HOUR

¼ cup melted butter or soft margarine
¾ cup firmly packed brown sugar
2 eggs
½ teaspoon pure lemon extract
1 cup finely chopped green tomatoes with juice
¼ cup fresh orange juice
2½ cups sifted unbleached all-purpose flour
1 tablespoon baking powder
½ teaspoon baking soda
½ teaspoon salt
½ cup candied fruit
2 tablespoons grated orange peel
½ cup chopped walnuts
1 cup whipped topping (optional)

Preheat oven to 350° F. In a medium-size bowl, cream together the butter, brown sugar, and eggs. Add the lemon extract, tomatoes, and orange juice. Mix well.

In a large bowl, mix the remaining dry ingredients and add alternately with the candied fruit, orange peel, and walnuts to the tomato mixture. Stir until well blended.

Pour the batter into an oiled bundt pan or ring-shaped cake pan. Bake for 40 minutes, or until a tester inserted in the center comes out clean. Cool for 10 minutes on a wire rack. Unmold onto a serving dish. Serve with the whipped topping, if desired.

Holiday Spice Bread

YIELD: 3 LOAVES
TIME: 1 HOUR 30 MINUTES

Why three loaves of bread? Freeze some loaves to bring out for the holidays, for busy days, or for delicious food gifts.

5 cups sifted unbleached all-purpose flour
5 teaspoons baking powder
2 teaspoons baking soda
1 teaspoon salt
2 cups firmly packed brown sugar
4 tablespoons ground cinnamon
2 teaspoons ground nutmeg
1 teaspoon ground ginger
1 teaspoon ground allspice
½ cup honey
1 cup vegetable oil
2 cups chopped green tomatoes
4 eggs
2 teaspoons pure vanilla extract
1 cup chopped walnuts
1½ cups raisins
2 tablespoons grated orange peel

Preheat oven to 350° F. In a large bowl, sift together all the dry ingredients. In another large bowl, mix the remaining ingredients and add to the dry ingredients. Beat well. Divide the batter among three oiled loaf pans. Bake for 45 minutes, or until a tester inserted in the center comes out clean. Cool for 10 minutes on a wire rack.

Green Tomato Bread

YIELD: 2 LOAVES
TIME: 1 HOUR 45 MINUTES

8-10 medium green tomatoes, coarsely chopped
⅔ cup raisins
⅔ cup boiling water
⅔ cup vegetable shortening
2⅔ cups sugar
4 eggs
3⅓ cups unbleached all-purpose flour
2 teaspoons baking soda
1½ teaspoons salt
½ teaspoon baking powder
1 teaspoon ground cinnamon
1 teaspoon ground cloves
⅔ cup coarsely chopped pecans or walnuts

Preheat oven to 350° F. In a blender or food processor, puree the tomatoes until smooth; you should have 2 cups pulp. Set aside. Soak the raisins in the boiling water and set aside to cool.

In a large bowl, cream together the shortening and sugar until fluffy. Add the eggs, reserved tomato pulp, and the plumped raisins and soaking water. Beat well.

In another large bowl, combine the flour, baking soda, salt, baking powder, cinnamon, cloves, and pecans. Add the flour mixture, one cup at a time, to the egg mixture, stirring well after each addition. Divide the batter into two oiled loaf pans and bake for 1 hour 10 minutes, or until a tester inserted in the center comes out clean. Cool for 10 minutes on a wire rack.

Sweet Green Tomato Muffins

YIELD: 12 MUFFINS
TIME: 45 MINUTES

2 cups sifted unbleached all-purpose flour
1 tablespoon baking powder
½ teaspoon salt
2 teaspoons ground cinnamon
1 egg
¼ cup vegetable oil
⅓ cup honey
1 cup low-fat milk
2 cups chopped green tomatoes
½ cup raisins

Preheat oven to 450° F. In a large bowl, sift together the flour, baking powder, salt, and cinnamon.

In a medium-size bowl, beat the egg and combine it with the remaining ingredients. Make a well in the center of the dry ingredients and pour the wet ingredients in with the dry ingredients all at once. Stir just enough to moisten the batter, about 15 strokes. The batter should look lumpy.

Oil the muffin cups or line with paper liners. Fill each cup two-thirds full of batter. Bake for 25 minutes or until well browned.

Cheesy Green Tomato Muffins

YIELD: 12 MUFFINS
TIME: 45 MINUTES

2 cups sifted unbleached all-purposed flour
1 tablespoon baking powder
½ teaspoon salt
1 egg
¼ cup vegetable oil
2 tablespoons honey
1 cup low-fat milk
2 cups chopped green tomatoes
1 cup grated low-fat cheddar cheese

Preheat oven to 450° F. In a large bowl, sift together the flour, baking powder, and salt. Make a well in the center of the bowl. Beat the egg and combine with the remaining ingredients. Pour the wet ingredients in with the dry ingredients all at once. Stir just enough to moisten the batter, about 15 strokes. The batter should look lumpy.

Oil the muffin cups or line with paper liners. Fill each cup two-thirds full of batter. Bake for 25 minutes or until well browned.

Oatmeal Cookie Bars

YIELD: 25 BARS
TIME: 1 HOUR

4 cups finely chopped green tomatoes
2 cups firmly packed dark brown sugar
2 tablespoons fresh lemon juice
1 teaspoon pure lemon extract
¾ cup butter or soft margarine
1½ cups unbleached all-purpose flour
½ teaspoon baking soda
½ teaspoon salt
2 cups rolled oats
½ cup chopped walnuts

Preheat oven to 375° F. In a large saucepan, combine the tomatoes with 1 cup brown sugar and the lemon juice. Simmer for 15-20 minutes, or until the tomato mixture is very thick. Remove from heat and stir in the lemon extract. Set aside.

In a large bowl, cream together the butter and remaining brown sugar until fluffy. Add the flour, baking soda, and salt. Mix well. Stir in the oats and walnuts.

Oil a 9 by 12-inch baking pan and press two-thirds of the oat mixture into the bottom. Next spread on the reserved tomato mixture. Sprinkle the remaining oat mixture over the top and bake for 30-35 minutes. Cool in the pan and cut into bars.

VARIATION: Two cups *Green Tomato Mincemeat without Meat* (see page 245) can be used instead of the green tomato mixture.

Old-Fashioned Filled Cookies

YIELD: 42 COOKIES
TIME: 1 HOUR PLUS CHILLING TIME

DOUGH:

1½ cups sugar
½ cup butter or soft margarine
1 egg, well beaten
½ cup low-fat milk
3½ cups unbleached all-purpose flour
2 teaspoons baking soda
2 teaspoons cream of tartar
½ teaspoons salt

FILLING:

½ cup sugar
1 tablespoon cornstarch
1½ cups chopped green tomatoes
Grated peel and juice of 1 lemon

In a large bowl, cream together the 1½ cups sugar and butter until fluffy. Add the egg and milk and blend well. In a small bowl, combine the flour, baking soda, cream of tartar, and salt. Add the flour mixture to the egg mixture and blend well. Chill for 1 hour.

In a large saucepan, combine the ½ cup sugar, cornstarch, and tomatoes. Cook on low heat, stirring constantly, until very thick. Add the lemon peel and juice and stir well. Heat again until bubbly. Chill.

Preheat oven to 350° F. To assemble cookies: Roll the chilled dough to ⅛-inch thickness and cut out the cookies with a cookie cutter. Top half of the cookies with 1 tablespoon of the chilled filling. Using a thimble, cut the center from the remaining half of the cut-out cookies and place on top of the filled halves. Crimp the edges with a fork to seal. Place the cookies on an oiled baking sheet and bake for 15-20 minutes or until lightly browned.

. . . .

Old-Time Bread Pudding

YIELD: 8 SERVINGS
TIME: 1 HOUR 30 MINUTES

●

6 tablespoons butter or soft margarine
12 slices whole wheat bread
1 cup *Green Tomato Mincemeat without Meat* (see page 245)
4 eggs
1¾ cups low-fat milk
½ cup pure maple syrup or honey

Preheat oven to 350° F. Butter the slices of bread on both sides. Line an oiled loaf pan with 8 slices of bread. Spread half of the mincemeat on top of the bread. Top with 2 slices of bread. Spread on the remaining mincemeat. Cover with the remaining bread.

In a medium-size bowl, beat the eggs and mix in the milk and maple syrup. Pour the milk mixture over everything. Bake for 1 hour, or until a knife inserted in the center comes out clean. Serve warm.

Coffeecake Twist

YIELD: 8 SERVINGS
TIME: 3 HOURS

⅓ cup low-fat milk
2 tablespoons active dry yeast
3⅓ cups sifted unbleached all-purpose flour
4 tablespoons melted butter or soft margarine
⅓ cup sugar
½ teaspoon salt
2 eggs
1 cup *Green Tomato Mincemeat without Meat* (see page 245)

In a small saucepan, heat the milk until just lukewarm. In a small bowl, mix the yeast and 2 tablespoons warm milk until smooth. Add the remaining warm milk.

In a large bowl, pour the flour and make a well in the center. Pour the milk mixture in the well and sprinkle a little flour over the mixture. Cover the bowl with a towel and set in a warm place for 15 minutes.

Combine the butter, sugar, salt, and eggs. Stir the reserved flour mixture and add the butter mixture. Stir until the flour mixture is well blended. On a lightly floured surface, knead the dough for 10 minutes or until smooth. Cover with a towel and let the dough rise in a warm place for 30-40 minutes.

Preheat oven to 400° F. Roll out the dough to form a rectangle 18 by 2-inches. Spread the mincemeat over the dough. Roll the dough lengthwise and seal the edges by pinching together. Cut the roll in half lengthwise and twist the pieces around each other to make a twisted roll. Place the twisted roll on an oiled baking sheet and let rise for 15 minutes. Bake for 30 minutes.

Sally's Green Tomato Fruit Cake

YIELD: 10 SERVINGS
TIME: 1 HOUR 30 MINUTES

2½ cups chopped green tomatoes
1 cup water
½ cup golden raisins
½ cup raisins
¾ cup chopped walnuts
½ cup butter or soft margarine
½ teaspoon ground nutmeg
½ teaspoon ground allspice
2 teaspoons ground cinnamon
1½ cups firmly packed brown sugar
1 teaspoon pure vanilla extract
2 cups sifted unbleached all-purpose flour
5 teaspoons baking powder
¼ cup confectioners' sugar
1½ cups whipped topping (optional)

Preheat oven to 350° F. In a medium-size saucepan, combine the tomatoes, water, raisins, walnuts, butter, spices, and brown sugar. Bring to boil. Reduce heat and simmer for 4 minutes. Cool to lukewarm. Add the vanilla extract.

Sift together the flour and baking powder and add to the tomato mixture. Beat well. Pour into an oiled 8 by 10-inch pan. Bake for 30-35 minutes, or until a tester inserted in the center comes out clean. Cool the cake on a wire rack, then invert on a serving plate. Dust with the confectioners' sugar and serve with the whipped topping.

Upside-Down Cake

YIELD: 12 SERVINGS
TIME: 1 HOUR

¾ cup butter or soft margarine
3 cups *Green Tomato Mincemeat without Meat* (see page 245)
1 cup low-fat milk
2 eggs, beaten
3 cups sifted unbleached all-purpose flour
4 teaspoons baking powder
½ teaspoon salt
1 cup sugar
2 teaspoons ground cinnamon

Preheat oven to 400° F. In a small saucepan, melt 4 tablespoons butter and pour into a bundt pan or ring-shaped cake pan. Coat the pan by tipping until it is buttered all over. Spread three-fourths of the mincemeat in the pan.

In the same saucepan, melt the remaining butter. Add the milk and eggs and mix well. In a large bowl, mix the dry ingredients. Add the dry ingredients to the wet ingredients and mix until smooth.

Pour half of the batter over the mincemeat and spread the remaining mincemeat evenly over the batter. Pour on the remaining batter. Bake for 35 minutes, or until a tester inserted in the center comes out clean. Cool the cake on a wire rack, then invert on a serving plate.

Andrea's Green Tomato Chocolate Cake

YIELD: 12-15 SERVINGS
TIME: 1 HOUR

⅔ cup butter or soft margarine
1¾ cups sugar
4 ounces unsweetened chocolate, melted
2 eggs
1 teaspoon pure vanilla extract
½ cup cocoa
2½ cups sifted unbleached all-purpose flour *or*
1½ cups sifted unbleached all-purpose flour and 1 cup whole wheat flour
2 teaspoons baking powder
2 teaspoons baking soda
¼ teaspoon salt
1 cup beer
1 cup pureed green tomatoes
¼-½ cup water (optional)

Preheat oven to 350° F. In a large bowl, cream together the butter and sugar. Stir in the chocolate, and then the eggs, one at a time. Add the vanilla extract.

In another large bowl, sift together the cocoa, flour, baking powder, baking soda, and salt. Add the flour mixture to the butter mixture alternately with the beer and tomatoes. If the batter appears stiff, add the water.

Pour the batter into an oiled and floured 9 by 13-inch baking pan. Bake for 35 minutes, or until a tester inserted in the center comes out clean. Cool the cake on a wire rack, then invert on a serving plate. Ice with your favorite frosting, or serve plain.

Surprising Brown Betty

YIELD: 6-8 SERVINGS
TIME: 1 HOUR 30 MINUTES

2 tablespoons butter or soft margarine
5 large green tomatoes, chopped
1 teaspoon ground cinnamon
1 teaspoon ground allspice
1 teaspoon ground nutmeg
½ cup raisins
Grated peel and juice of 1 lemon
1 cup firmly packed brown sugar
½ cup butter or soft margarine
1 cup bread crumbs
1 cup wheat germ

Preheat oven to 350° F. In a large saucepan, melt the 2 tablespoons butter and add the tomatoes, spices, raisins, and lemon peel. Stir in the brown sugar.

In a medium-size saucepan, melt the ½ cup butter. Add the bread crumbs and wheat germ and mix well.

Oil a covered baking dish and put in half of the crumb mixture. Add the tomato mixture and squeeze the juice of the lemon over the tomato mixture. Sprinkle on the remaining crumb mixture. Cover and bake for 40 minutes. Remove the cover and bake for 10 minutes more. Serve warm.

Green Tomato Pie

YIELD: 6 SERVINGS
TIME: 1 HOUR

Pastry for two 9-inch pie crusts
3 large green tomatoes, cut into ½-inch cubes
Pinch salt
1 tablespoon unbleached all-purpose flour
1 cup sugar
1 tablespoon fresh lemon juice
1 tablespoon butter or soft margarine
1 teaspoon ground cinnamon
¼ teaspoon ground nutmeg

Preheat oven to 350° F. Line a 9-inch pie pan with half the pastry. Roll out the remaining pastry for the top and cut four 1-inch slits in the center.

In a medium-size bowl, combine the remaining ingredients and fill the pie crust. Top with the rolled-out pastry and crimp the edges to seal. Bake for 45 minutes. Serve warm.

Green Tomato Custard Pie

YIELD: 8 SERVINGS
TIME: 1 HOUR PLUS CHILLING TIME

Pastry for one 10-inch pie crust
5 eggs
½ cup sugar
¼ cup pure maple syrup
2 teaspoons cider vinegar
½ teaspoon salt
½ teaspoon ground cinnamon
¾ cup green tomato puree (see page 279)
2 cups warm low-fat milk

Preheat oven to 425° F. Line a 10-inch pie pan with the pastry and flute the edges. Prick the crust with a fork and bake for 15 minutes. Remove the crust from the oven and reduce heat to 350° F.

Beat together the eggs, sugar, maple syrup, vinegar, salt, and cinnamon. Slowly add the tomato puree and warm milk, stirring constantly. Pour the custard mixture into the baked crust and bake for 30 minutes, or until a knife inserted in the center comes out clean. Chill for 30 minutes before serving.

Candied Green Tomato Bits

YIELD: 1½-2 CUPS
TIME: 1 HOUR 10 MINUTES

Use these tomato bits in fruit cakes, candies, cookies, or in any way you would use candied fruit.

4 medium green tomatoes
2 cups sugar
1 cup water
Sugar

Cut the tomatoes into quarters. Scoop out the seeds and pulp and discard. Cut the fleshy outer shell into small pieces and drain thoroughly.

In a large skillet, combine the 2 cups sugar and water and bring to a boil. Reduce heat and cook to the soft ball stage (238° F.).

Slowly add half the tomato pieces and simmer until clear. Remove the tomato pieces and drain. Reheat the sugar mixture to boiling and drop in the remaining tomato pieces. Repeat.

When all the tomato pieces are cooked and drained, roll in sugar. Store in rigid plastic containers. The tomato bits will keep for several months in the refrigerator or may be frozen.

Easy Green Tomato Dills

YIELD: 1 QUART
TIME: 20 MINUTES

●

This recipe is given for one quart, but easily can be increased to accommodate all your green cherry tomatoes. This recipe does not call for processing, so you should store the pickles in the refrigerator after opening.

2 pounds green cherry tomatoes
1 clove garlic
½ teaspoon mixed pickling spices
1 fresh dill head
1 small piece hot red chile pepper (optional)
2 quarts water
2 cups white vinegar
1 cup pickling salt

Stem the tomatoes, but do *not* peel or core. Loosely pack the tomatoes in a sterilized quart jar. Add the garlic, pickling spices, dill head, and chile.

In a medium-size saucepan, combine the water, vinegar, and salt. Bring to a boil and stir to dissolve the salt. Pour the vinegar mixture over the tomatoes, leaving a ½-inch headspace. Seal according to manufacturer's directions. Allow six weeks to cure before serving. Keep refrigerated.

Mustard Jumble

YIELD: 6-7 QUARTS
TIME: 2 HOURS 30 MINUTES PLUS STANDING TIME

This is the pickle to make at the height of the season when you are inundated with garden surplus.

6 pounds green tomatoes, cored and coarsely chopped
4 medium cucumbers, unpeeled and diced
4 small zucchini, unpeeled and diced
1 large head cauliflower, cut into small florets
1 bunch celery, diced on the diagonal
6 medium red bell peppers, cored, seeded, and coarsely chopped
2 pounds carrots, cut into ¼-inch slices
2 pounds pearl onions, peeled
1½ cups pickling salt
⅔ cup cider vinegar
4 cups sugar
1 cup unbleached all-purpose flour
4 tablespoons Dijon mustard
2 tablespoons ground turmeric
¼ teaspoon cayenne powder
1 cup white vinegar

In a large stainless steel or porcelain bowl, combine all the vegetables. Sprinkle with the salt and mix well. Cover loosely with a towel. Let stand overnight.

Drain the vegetables. In a large saucepan, cover the vegetables with water and bring to a boil. Boil for 15 minutes. Drain again.

In a large stainless steel or enameled pot, heat the cider vinegar and sugar. In a small bowl, mix together the flour, mustard, spices, and the white vinegar to form a smooth paste. Add the paste to the cider vinegar mixture. Add the vegetables and heat to boiling.

Fill hot, sterilized quart jars with the tomato mixture, leaving a ½-inch headspace. Seal and process in a boiling water bath for 10 minutes. (See pages 276-277.)

. . . .

Dilled Green Cherries

YIELD: 6 QUARTS
TIME: 45 MINUTES

●

12 pounds green cherry tomatoes

2 cups white vinegar

¾ cup pickling salt

4 tablespoons mixed pickling spices in a muslin bag

2 quarts water

12 grape leaves

6 cloves garlic

24 black peppercorns

6 fresh dill heads

Stem all the tomatoes, but do *not* peel or core. In a large stainless steel or enameled pot, heat the vinegar, salt, pickling spices, and water to a boil. Reduce heat and simmer for 15 minutes. Remove the spice bag.

In the bottom of each hot, sterilized quart jar, place 2 grape leaves, 1 clove garlic, 4 peppercorns, and 1 dill head. Fill the jars with the tomatoes. Pour the vinegar mixture over the tomatoes, leaving a ½-inch headspace. Seal and process in a boiling water bath for 10 minutes. (See pages 276-277.) Allow six weeks to cure before serving.

French Pickles

YIELD: 6 PINTS
TIME: 1 HOUR PLUS STANDING TIME

11 pounds green tomatoes, cored and cut into ¼-inch slices
3 large onions, thinly sliced
½ cup pickling salt
2 cups white vinegar
3 cups packed brown sugar
½ cup white mustard seeds
½ teaspoon ground cloves
½ teaspoon ground ginger
1 teaspoon ground mustard
¼ teaspoon cayenne powder

In a large stainless steel or porcelain bowl, combine the tomatoes and onions. Sprinkle with the salt and mix well. Cover loosely with a towel. Let stand for 12 hours. Drain well and discard liquid.

In a large stainless steel or enameled pot, add the remaining ingredients and simmer for 15 minutes. Then bring the mixture to a boil.

Fill hot, sterilized pint jars with the tomatoes and onions. Pour the hot vinegar mixture over the slices, leaving a ½-inch headspace. Seal and process in a boiling water bath for 10 minutes. (See pages 276-277.)

Sweet Green Wheels

YIELD: 10 PINTS
TIME: 1 HOUR 30 MINUTES PLUS SOAKING TIME

12-13 pounds green tomatoes, cored and cut into ¼-inch slices
10 small onions, cut into ¼-inch slices
2 quarts water
½ cup pickling salt
3 cups water
1 cup cider vinegar
2 cinnamon sticks
1 teaspoon whole cloves
2 tablespoons mixed pickling spices
1 quart cider vinegar
3 cups honey

In a large stainless steel or porcelain bowl, layer the tomatoes and onions. Combine the 2 quarts water and salt. Pour the water mixture over the tomato mixture. Let soak overnight. Cover loosely with a towel. Drain the tomato mixture and rinse well in cold water.

In a large stainless steel or enameled pot, combine the tomato mixture with the 3 cups water and the 1 cup vinegar. Simmer for 1 hour or until light in color.

In a muslin spice bag, combine the cinnamon sticks, cloves, and pickling spices. In a large saucepan, combine the 1 quart vinegar, honey, and spice bag and bring to a boil. Boil for 10 minutes. Remove the spice bag.

Fill hot, sterilized pint jars with the tomato mixture. Pour the hot honey mixture over the tomato mixture, leaving a ½-inch headspace. Seal and process in a boiling water bath for 10 minutes. (See pages 276-277.)

Sweet Pickle Relish

YIELD: 12 PINTS
TIME: 2 HOURS PLUS STANDING TIME

8 pounds green tomatoes, cored
2 medium onions
4 medium green bell peppers, cored and seeded
2 medium red bell peppers, cored and seeded
½ cup pickling salt
1 teaspoon mixed pickling spices in a muslin bag
1 tablespoon celery seeds
3 cinnamon sticks
3 cups white vinegar
1 cup water
2 cups sugar

In a blender or food processor, coarsely chop all the vegetables. In a large stainless steel or porcelain bowl, combine all the vegetables. Sprinkle with the salt and mix well. Cover loosely with a towel. Let stand overnight. Drain well and discard liquid.

In a large stainless steel or enameled pot, combine the vegetables with the remaining ingredients. Simmer for 30 minutes, stirring occasionally. Remove the spice bag and cinnamon sticks.

Fill hot, sterilized pint jars with the vegetable mixture, leaving a ½-inch headspace. Seal and process in a boiling water bath for 10 minutes. (See pages 276-277.)

Chinese Tomato Relish

YIELD: 4 QUARTS
TIME: 45 MINUTES

3 cups cider vinegar
2 cups firmly packed brown sugar
2 tablespoons pickling salt
1 tablespoon ground ginger
1 teaspoon ground nutmeg
2 teaspoons ground coriander
4 tablespoons mixed pickling spices in a muslin bag
10 pounds barely ripe (pink-green) tomatoes, cored and cut into 1-inch chunks
1 bunch celery, diced
1 large onion, coarsely chopped
4 cloves garlic, minced
⅓ cup cornstarch
1 cup cold water

In a large stainless steel or enameled pot, combine the vinegar, brown sugar, salt, ginger, nutmeg, and coriander. Add the spice bag and bring to a boil. Boil for 5 minutes. Add the tomatoes, celery, onion, and garlic and mix well.

In a small bowl, mix the cornstarch and water, stirring constantly to prevent lumps. Add the cornstarch mixture to the tomato mixture and continue boiling for 10 minutes more. Remove the spice bag.

Fill hot, sterilized quart jars with the tomato mixture, leaving a ½-inch headspace. Seal and process in a boiling water bath for 10 minutes. (See pages 276-277.)

Piccalilli

YIELD: 10 PINTS
. TIME: 2 HOURS PLUS SOAKING TIME

6 pounds green tomatoes, cored and coarsely chopped
3 tablespoons pickling salt
8 cups finely chopped green cabbage
2 cups chopped red bell peppers
1 large onion, finely chopped
4½ cups cider vinegar
2½ cups honey
2 teaspoons celery seeds
8 cardamom seeds
2 teaspoons ground allspice
2 teaspoons mustard seeds
2 teaspoons ground cinnamon

In a large stainless steel or porcelain bowl, place the tomatoes. Sprinkle with the salt and mix well. Cover loosely with a towel. Let stand overnight. Drain well and discard liquid.

In a large stainless steel or enameled pot, combine the tomatoes with the cabbage, bell peppers, onion, vinegar, and honey. Simmer for 30 minutes.

In a muslin spice bag, combine the celery seeds, cardamom seeds, allspice, and mustard seeds. Add the spice bag and cinnamon to the pot and simmer for 1 hour or until thick.

Fill hot, sterilized pint jars with the tomato mixture, leaving a ½-inch headspace. Seal and process in a boiling water bath for 5 minutes. (See pages 276-277.)

Chow-Chow

YIELD: 6-8 PINTS
TIME: 2 HOURS PLUS STANDING TIME

5 pounds green tomatoes, cored
1 medium head green cabbage
6 medium onions
6 medium green bell peppers, cored and seeded
6 medium red bell peppers, cored and seeded
¼ cup pickling salt
2 tablespoons prepared mustard
6 cups white vinegar
2½ cups sugar
1½ teaspoons ground turmeric
1 teaspoon ground ginger
2 tablespoons mustard seeds
1 tablespoon celery seeds
1 tablespoon mixed pickling spices in a muslin bag

In a blender or food processor, coarsely chop all the vegetables. In a large stainless steel or porcelain bowl, combine all the vegetables with the salt and mix well. Cover loosely with a towel. Let stand overnight. Drain well and discard liquid.

In a large stainless steel or enameled pot, blend together the prepared mustard, vinegar, sugar, and spices. Simmer for 2 minutes. Strain, then add the vegetables. Simmer for 10 minutes more. Remove the spice bag.

Fill the hot, sterilized pint jars with the vegetable mixture, leaving a ½-inch headspace. Seal and process in a boiling water bath for 10 minutes. (See pages 276-277.) Use within six months.

Pennsylvania Chow-Chow

YIELD: 10-11 PINTS
TIME: 2 HOURS PLUS STANDING TIME

10 pounds green tomatoes, cored and finely chopped
3 cups finely chopped red bell peppers
6 pounds onions, finely chopped
½ cup pickling salt
5 cups cider vinegar
2 cups sugar
2 cups honey
½ cup cornstarch
1 teaspoon ground mustard
1 teaspoon ground turmeric
1 teaspoon curry powder
⅓ cup cider vinegar

In a large stainless steel or porcelain bowl, combine all the vegetables. Sprinkle with the salt and mix well. Cover loosely with a towel. Let stand overnight. Drain well and discard liquid.

In a large stainless steel or enameled pot, combine the vegetables with the 5 cups vinegar and the sugar and honey. Cook for 1 hour on medium heat, stirring occasionally.

In a small bowl, make a paste with the cornstarch, mustard, turmeric, curry powder, and the ⅓ cup vinegar. Blend the paste into the vegetables and cook on low heat for 15 minutes or until very thick.

Fill hot, sterilized pint jars with the vegetable mixture, leaving a ½-inch headspace. Seal and process in a boiling water bath for 5 minutes. (See pages 276-277.)

Green Tomato Mincemeat without Meat

YIELD: 10 PINTS
TIME: 3 HOURS

8 cups finely chopped green tomatoes
1-1½ cups apple cider
8 cups finely chopped unpeeled apples
1½ pounds raisins
1 pound dates, chopped
2 cups honey
1⅓ cups cider vinegar
2 tablespoons ground cinnamon
1 teaspoon ground allspice
2 teaspoons ground cloves
¼ teaspoon freshly ground black pepper
2 tablespoons orange peel
⅔ cup vegetable oil

Drain the tomatoes for 5-10 minutes. Replace the juice with the same amount of the apple cider.

In a large stainless steel or enameled pot, combine the tomatoes and cider with the remaining ingredients, except the oil. Simmer for 2 hours or until thick. Add the oil and stir well.

Fill hot, sterilized pint jars with the tomato mixture, leaving a ½-inch headspace. Seal and process in a boiling water bath for 25 minutes. (See pages 276-277.) You can also freeze the mincemeat.

Teatime Marmalade

YIELD: 8 HALF-PINT JARS
TIME: 2 HOURS

3 lemons
½ cup water
5 pounds green tomatoes, cored, peeled, and thinly sliced
4 cups granulated sugar
1 cup firmly packed light brown sugar
1 tablespoon canning salt
2 cinnamon sticks

Peel the skin off one lemon in thin strips, removing as much of the white membrane as possible. Cut the lemon peel strips into tiny slivers.

In a small saucepan, boil the water and add the lemon peel slivers. Reduce heat and simmer for 10 minutes. Drain. Trim off all the white membrane on the remaining lemons and cut into very thin slices. Quarter the slices and remove the seeds.

In a large stainless steel or enameled pot, combine the lemon peel slivers, lemon quarters, tomatoes, sugars, salt, and cinnamon. Cook, uncovered, on medium heat for 50 minutes or until very thick, stirring occasionally. Remove the cinnamon sticks.

Fill hot, sterilized half-pint jars with the tomato mixture, leaving a ¼-inch headspace. Seal according to manufacturer's directions.

Green Tomato Marmalade

YIELD: 6 PINTS
TIME: 2 HOURS 15 MINUTES PLUS STANDING TIME

4 oranges
8 pounds green tomatoes, cored, peeled, and thinly sliced
3½ pounds sugar

Peel the skin off the oranges in thin strips, removing as much of the white membrane as possible. Cut the orange peel strips into thinner strips. Cut the orange into thin slices.

In a large stainless steel or porcelain bowl, combine the tomatoes, orange peel strips, and orange slices with the sugar and mix well. Cover loosely with a towel. Let stand overnight.

In a large stainless steel or enameled pot, bring the tomato mixture gradually to a boil, stirring occasionally. Reduce heat and simmer for 2 hours or until thick.

Fill hot, sterilized pint jars with the tomato mixture, leaving a ¼-inch headspace. Seal according to manufacturer's directions.

Green Tomato Butter

YIELD: 4 PINTS
TIME: 3 HOURS

6 pounds green tomatoes, stemmed and coarsely chopped
2 tablespoons ground ginger
2 teaspoons ground cinnamon
1 teaspoon ground allspice
5 pounds brown sugar
Juice of 2 lemons
2 cups water

In a large stainless steel or enameled pot, combine the tomatoes with the remaining ingredients. Simmer for 2-3 hours or until thick, stirring frequently. Strain and reheat to boiling.

Fill hot, sterilized pint jars with the tomato mixture, leaving a ¼-inch headspace. Seal according to manufacturer's directions.

Green Tomato Preserves

YIELD: 6 PINTS
TIME: 2 HOURS PLUS STANDING TIME

5 pounds green tomatoes, cored, peeled, and finely chopped
4 pounds sugar
2 lemons, thinly sliced with peel

In a large stainless steel or porcelain bowl, combine the tomatoes and sugar and mix well. Cover loosely with a towel. Let stand overnight.

In a large stainless steel or enameled pot, drain the liquid from the tomatoes and boil the liquid until thick. Add the tomatoes and lemon slices and cook until thick and clear. Reheat to boiling.

Fill hot, sterilized pint jars with the tomato mixture, leaving a ¼-inch headspace. Seal according to manufacturer's directions.

4

Red & Green Together

Red, White & Green Soup

YIELD: 10 SERVINGS
TIME: 1 HOUR

3 tablespoons butter or soft margarine
2 tablespoons vegetable oil
4 very large onions, sliced into rings
5 medium red tomatoes, diced
4 medium green tomatoes, diced
⅓ cup unbleached all-purpose flour
2 teaspoons ground mustard
1 cup dry red wine
6 cups beef or vegetable broth
2 teaspoons dried basil
2 teaspoons ground paprika
Salt and freshly ground black pepper to taste
2 eggs, beaten
Grated Parmesan cheese

In a large pot, melt the butter with the oil and sauté the onion rings for 15 minutes or until tender and beginning to brown. Add the tomatoes and continue cooking for 5 minutes. Stir in the flour and mustard. Add the wine and stir slowly. Add the broth, basil, paprika, salt, and pepper. Simmer for 30 minutes.

Just before serving, add 1 cup of hot soup to the beaten eggs and mix well. (When you mix egg yolks into a hot mixture, it is important to warm them a bit before adding to the mixture.) Add the egg mixture to the pot and heat through, but do not boil or the soup will curdle. Serve garnished with the cheese.

October Lentil Soup

YIELD: 8 SERVINGS
TIME: 1 HOUR 30 MINUTES

●

2 tablespoons vegetable oil
1 medium onion, diced
1 clove garlic, minced
2 stalks celery, diced
2 large carrots, diced
3 large green tomatoes, diced
1½ cups lentils
5 cups water
1 teaspoon dried thyme
½ teaspoon dried oregano
1 teaspoon dried basil
4 cups chopped red tomatoes
3 tablespoons tomato paste (optional)
Salt and freshly ground black pepper to taste
¼ cup dry sherry
1 cup low-fat sour cream

In a large pot, heat the oil and sauté the onion, garlic, celery, carrots, and tomatoes for 10 minutes, stirring frequently. Add the remaining ingredients, except the sherry and sour cream, and bring to a boil. Cover and simmer for 1 hour, or until the lentils are tender. Put half the lentil mixture in a blender or food processor and blend until smooth. Return the lentil puree to the pot. Add the sherry and cook for 10 minutes, uncovered. Garnish with the sour cream and serve.

Mulligatawny Soup

YIELD: 8 SERVINGS
TIME: 1 HOUR 30 MINUTES

Mulligatawny soup is traditionally served as a smooth soup with pieces of chicken in it. This recipe has chunky vegetable pieces. If you would like a smooth soup, puree the vegetables with a little broth after being sautéed, and continue with the recipe.

2 tablespoons vegetable oil
1 medium onion, diced
1 medium carrot, diced
2 stalks celery, diced
1 cup diced turnips
4 medium green tomatoes, diced
6 cups chicken broth
¼ cup tomato paste
2 teaspoons curry powder
Dash cayenne powder
½ cup unbleached all-purpose flour
2 cups cooked diced chicken
2 cups cooked chick-peas
Salt and freshly ground black pepper to taste
½ cup shredded coconut

In a large pot, heat the oil and sauté the onion, carrot, celery, turnips, and tomatoes for 10 minutes, or until the vegetables are softened slightly. Add 5 cups chicken broth, the tomato paste, curry powder, and cayenne powder.

In a small bowl, mix the flour and the remaining chicken broth. Stir the paste into the soup. Add the remaining ingredients, except the coconut, and simmer for 1 hour. Garnish with the coconut and serve.

Green Tomato Medley

YIELD: 6 SERVINGS
TIME: 30 MINUTES PLUS CHILLING TIME

¼ cup vegetable oil
3 medium green tomatoes, cored, peeled, and cut into 1-inch cubes
3 medium zucchini, unpeeled and cut into 1-inch cubes
¼ pound fresh mushrooms, sliced
¾ cup chopped onions
½ cup sliced celery
1 clove garlic, minced
¼ cup red wine vinegar
1 tablespoon sugar
½ teaspoon salt
⅛ teaspoon freshly ground black pepper
1 cup chopped red tomatoes
¼ cup sliced green olives

In a large skillet, heat the oil and stir-fry the green tomatoes, zucchini, mushrooms, onions, celery, and garlic for 10 minutes or until tender crisp. Add the vinegar, sugar, salt, and pepper. Reduce heat, cover, and simmer for 5 minutes.

Stir in the red tomatoes and olives and bring to a boil. Remove from heat and place in a large bowl. Chill for 1 hour and serve.

Green Tomato Caponata

YIELD: 8 SERVINGS
TIME: 45 MINUTES PLUS CHILLING TIME

The secret of this dish is that each vegetable is sautéed separately to retain its flavor. Serve with Italian bread, or stuffed in tomatoes or pita bread.

½ cup olive oil
2 cups diced celery
1 large onion, diced
6 cups unpeeled cubed eggplant
4 medium green tomatoes, diced
½ cup red wine vinegar
½ cup water
1 teaspoon honey
¼ cup tomato paste
2 tablespoons capers
½ cup minced fresh parsley
Salt and freshly ground black pepper to taste

In a large skillet, heat 3 tablespoons oil and sauté the celery until just tender. Do *not* brown. Remove the celery to a large bowl. Add 2 tablespoons oil to the skillet and sauté the onion. Add the onion to the celery.

Heat the remaining oil and sauté the eggplant for 5 minutes. Add the tomatoes and cook the tomatoes until soft. Remove the vegetable mixture from the skillet and add to the celery and onion. Leave the liquid in the skillet. Add the vinegar, water, honey, tomato paste, and capers. Simmer for 5 minutes.

Return the vegetable mixture to the skillet, add the parsley, and simmer for 10 minutes. Add the salt and pepper. Chill completely before serving. Caponata keeps well in the refrigerator for several days.

Spanish Rice

YIELD: 6-8 SERVINGS
TIME: 30-45 MINUTES

2 cups tomato juice or puree
2 cups water *or* chicken or vegetable broth
2 cups uncooked white or brown rice
2 tablespoons vegetable oil
1 medium onion, minced
1 stalk celery, minced
1 small green bell pepper, minced
1 medium green tomato, minced

In a large saucepan, heat the tomato juice and water to a boil. Add the rice and cook until tender — 15 minutes for white rice, 45 minutes for brown rice.

In a medium-size skillet, heat the oil and sauté the vegetables for 10 minutes. When the rice is cooked, stir in the vegetables and serve.

Tasty Stacks

YIELD: 4-6 SERVINGS
TIME: 1 HOUR

½ cup unbleached all-purpose flour
½ teaspoon salt
4 medium green tomatoes, cut into ¼-inch slices
1 egg, well beaten
6 tablespoons vegetable oil
12 slices American cheese
1 tablespoon vegetable oil
4 tablespoons minced onions
1 cup tomato sauce
1 teaspoon sugar
½ teaspoon salt

Preheat oven to 350° F. In a small bowl, combine the flour and salt. Dip the tomato slices into the egg, then into the flour mixture. In a medium-size skillet, heat the 6 tablespoons oil and sauté the tomato slices until browned. In a shallow baking dish, alternate the tomato slices with the cheese slices. Set aside.

In a large skillet, heat the 1 tablespoon oil and sauté the onions until translucent. Add the tomato sauce, sugar, and salt and heat to boiling. Remove from heat and pour the onion mixture over the reserved tomato slices. Bake for 30 minutes, or until the cheese is melted and lightly browned on top. Serve immediately.

Tomatoes in Hot Green Tomato Sauce

YIELD: 4 SERVINGS
TIME: 10 MINUTES

2 scallions, coarsely chopped
1 medium green tomato, quartered
1 tablespoon coarsely chopped fresh parsley
1 tablespoon low-fat cottage cheese
1 clove garlic, crushed
¼ small fresh or dried chile pepper *or* ¼ teaspoon chile sauce
Salt and freshly ground black pepper to taste
6 medium red tomatoes, quartered

In a blender or food processor, combine the scallions and green tomato. Add the remaining ingredients, except the red tomatoes, and blend for 15 seconds. Pour the sauce over the red tomato quarters and mix well. Serve hot or cold.

Enchilada Bake

YIELD: 6 SERVINGS
TIME: 1 HOUR 15 MINUTES

2 tablespoons vegetable oil
1 medium onion, diced
2 cloves garlic, minced
3 medium green tomatoes, diced
2 cups cooked red kidney beans
Salt and freshly ground black pepper to taste
3 tablespoons chile powder
12 soft corn tortillas
3 cups *Red Taco Sauce* (see page 118)
2 cups grated low-fat cheddar or Monterey Jack cheese

Preheat oven to 350° F. In a medium-size saucepan, heat the oil and sauté the onion, garlic, and tomatoes for 10 minutes. Add the kidney beans, salt, pepper, and chile powder. Mash half of the beans with the back of a spoon. Cook for 10 minutes more, stirring occasionally.

Oil a baking dish and line it with half of the tortillas. Spread half of the bean mixture on top of the tortillas and cover with half of the *Red Taco Sauce* and half of the cheese. Continue layering, ending with a layer of cheese. Bake for 45 minutes. Cut into squares and serve.

Sweet & Sour Chicken

YIELD: 6 SERVINGS
TIME: 1 HOUR 30 MINUTES

●

2 tablespoons butter or soft margarine
2 tablespoons vegetable oil
6 pieces chicken, skinned
4 medium green tomatoes, coarsely diced
1 medium carrot, sliced
1 medium green bell pepper, cored, seeded, and coarsely diced
1 medium onion, diced
2½ cups *Sweet & Sour Sauce* (see page 120)

Preheat oven to 350° F. In a large skillet, melt the butter with the oil and brown the chicken on both sides. Drain off the fat. Put the chicken into a baking dish and arrange the vegetables around the chicken. Pour the *Sweet & Sour Sauce* over the top and bake for 45-60 minutes. Serve immediately.

Stuffed Meat Loaf

YIELD: 6-8 SERVINGS
TIME: 1 HOUR 45 MINUTES

●

This is best when served with Celery Tomato Sauce (see page 121).

MEAT LOAF:

1½ pounds lean ground beef
2 eggs
1 medium onion, finely diced
2 cloves garlic, minced
¾ cup bread crumbs
½ cup tomato sauce, puree, or catsup
2 tablespoons Worcestershire sauce
1 teaspoon salt

STUFFING:

2 tablespoons vegetable oil
1 small onion, diced
2 large green tomatoes, diced
2 stalks celery, diced
2 medium carrots, diced
1 cup peas, fresh or frozen
1½ teaspoons dried basil
1 teaspoon dried thyme
½ cup grated Parmesan cheese
½ cup bread crumbs
Salt and freshly ground black pepper to taste

Preheat oven to 350° F. In a large mixing bowl, mix together all the ingredients for the meat loaf. Spread the meat mixture in the shape of a rectangle ½ inch thick on a piece of wax paper.

Heat the oil and sauté the onion, tomatoes, celery, and carrots for 10 minutes. Add the remaining ingredients. Spread the vegetable mixture over the meat loaf rectangle. Using the wax paper, roll the meat loaf in jelly-roll fashion. Place the meat loaf, seam side down, in a baking pan and bake for 1 hour. Serve hot.

. . . .

Spanish Casserole

YIELD: 6 SERVINGS
TIME: 1 HOUR

●

1 pound lean ground beef
1 small onion, minced
1 tablespoon chopped green bell pepper
1 tablespoon chopped red bell pepper
3 large green tomatoes, thickly sliced
¼ teaspoon garlic powder
¼ teaspoon ground cumin
Dash cayenne powder
1 cup tomato sauce
1½ cups cooked whole kernel corn

Preheat oven to 350° F. In a large skillet, sauté the ground beef, onion, and bell peppers until the meat is browned. Drain off the fat. Add the remaining ingredients and mix well. Pour into an oiled baking dish and bake for 35-45 minutes. Serve.

Simmering Chicken Pot

YIELD: 6 SERVINGS
TIME: 1 HOUR 30 MINUTES

This is delicious served over Yellow Confetti Rice (see page 204).

4 tablespoons vegetable oil
6 pieces chicken, skinned
2 cloves garlic, minced
1 medium onion, sliced into rings
1 medium green bell pepper, cored, seeded, and chopped
½ pound fresh mushrooms, sliced
6 medium green tomatoes, coarsely chopped
2 medium red tomatoes, coarsely chopped
1½ cups chicken broth
½ cup white wine (optional)
2 teaspoons dried thyme
1 teaspoon dried marjoram
Salt and freshly ground black pepper to taste
¾ cup unbleached all-purpose flour

In a large pot, heat 2 tablespoons oil and brown the chicken on both sides until just golden. Drain off the fat. Remove the chicken and set aside.

In the same pot, heat the remaining oil and sauté the garlic, onion, green pepper, and mushrooms for 5 minutes. Add the remaining ingredients, except the flour, and cook for 10 minutes. Return the chicken pieces to the pot. Ladle the sauce on each piece. Cover and simmer for 1 hour.

Twenty minutes before serving, remove the chicken from the pot and keep warm. In a small mixing bowl, blend the flour and 1 cup hot broth from the pot. Stir briskly to prevent lumps. Add the flour mixture to the pot and stir well. Return the chicken to the pot and cover. Simmer the mixture gently until ready to serve.

. . . .

Hectic Day Casserole

YIELD: 6 SERVINGS
TIME: 1 HOUR

1 pound lean ground beef
1 small onion, chopped
1 small green bell pepper, cored, seeded, and chopped
1 clove garlic, minced
1 teaspoon salt
2 cups tomato sauce
4 medium green tomatoes, cut into ¼-inch slices
1 cup shredded low-fat cheddar cheese

Preheat oven to 350° F. In a large skillet, sauté the ground beef, onion, green pepper, and garlic until the meat is browned. Drain off the fat. Add the salt and tomato sauce and cook on low heat for 15-20 minutes or until thick. Set aside.

Spread half of the tomato slices in an oiled baking dish, top with half of the cheese, then with half of the reserved meat mixture. Repeat the layers. Bake for 30 minutes. Serve.

Red & Green Parmigian

YIELD: 6 SERVINGS
TIME: 1 HOUR

½ cup unbleached all-purpose flour
½ teaspoon salt
6 medium green tomatoes, cut into ¼-inch slices
1 egg, well beaten
¼ cup vegetable oil
2 cups tomato sauce
¼ teaspoon dried oregano
1 teaspoon sugar
½ cup grated Parmesan cheese
½ pound shredded low-fat mozzarella cheese

Preheat oven to 350° F. In a small bowl, combine the flour and salt. Dip the tomato slices into the egg, then into the flour mixture. In a large skillet, heat the oil and sauté the tomato slices until browned. Drain on paper towels until all slices are cooked.

In a small bowl, combine the tomato sauce with the oregano and sugar. In a shallow baking dish, arrange half of the tomato slices. Pour half of the tomato mixture over the tomato slices. Sprinkle with half of the Parmesan cheese, then half of the mozzarella cheese. Repeat layers. Bake for 25-30 minutes or until bubbly and golden brown. Serve.

Tamale Pie

YIELD: 4-6 SERVINGS
TIME: 1 HOUR 15 MINUTES

1 cup yellow cornmeal
½ cup cold water
2½ cups boiling water
4 tablespoons vegetable oil
1 pound lean ground beef
1 medium onion, chopped
1 small green bell pepper, cored, seeded, and chopped
1 cup chopped green tomatoes
2 mild chile peppers, seeded and chopped
1 cup chopped red tomatoes
1 teaspoon ground cumin
Chile powder to taste
Salt and freshly ground black pepper to taste

Preheat oven to 350° F. In a small bowl, mix the cornmeal with the cold water. Slowly add the cornmeal mixture to the boiling water and cook for 15 minutes on low heat, stirring frequently. Set aside.

In a large skillet, heat 2 tablespoons oil and sauté the ground beef, onion, and green pepper until the meat is browned. Drain off the fat. Set aside.

In the same skillet, heat the remaining oil and add the green tomatoes and chile peppers. Cook until lightly browned, stirring frequently. Add the red tomatoes, cumin, chile powder, salt, and pepper and simmer for 10 minutes.

In an oiled baking dish, alternate layers of the reserved cornmeal mixture and meat mixture, and the tomato mixture and bake for 30 minutes. Serve hot.

Indian Pickles

YIELD: 5-6 PINTS
TIME: 1 HOUR PLUS SOAKING TIME

8 medium green tomatoes, cored
8 medium red tomatoes, cored and peeled
3 medium onions
3 medium red bell peppers, cored and seeded
1 large cucumber, unpeeled
7 cups chopped celery
⅔ cup pickling salt
6 cups white vinegar
6 cups firmly packed brown sugar
1 teaspoon ground mustard
1 teaspoon freshly ground white pepper

In a blender or food processor, coarsely chop all the vegetables. In a large stainless steel or porcelain bowl, layer the vegetables. Sprinkle with the salt and mix well. Let stand overnight. Drain well and discard liquid.

In a large stainless steel or enameled pot, combine the vegetables with the remaining ingredients. Place on low heat and slowly bring to a simmer. Cook for 30 minutes, stirring occasionally.

Fill hot, sterilized pint jars with the tomato mixture, leaving a ½-inch headspace. Seal and process in a boiling water bath for 10 minutes. (See pages 276-277.)

5

Growing, Preserving & Preparing Tips

Growing Tips

Even if you have never gardened before, you can expect success with tomatoes. They can be grown in every part of the country — in large fields, or in gardens as small as a pot on a balcony.

Growing your own tomatoes enables you to choose your varieties. As a gardener, you have many more types of tomatoes available to you than shoppers at a supermarket (who rarely get a vine-ripened tomato).

Italian plum tomatoes are especially good for sauces and purees because they have more pulp and less water than other tomatoes. Cherry tomatoes are great in salads, on vegetable platters, and as stuffed appetizers. And no garden is complete without an all-round, sweet, juicy, slicing tomato — terrific for eating fresh right from the garden or combined with other flavors in a cooked dish.

Choosing the best varieties to grow depends on the length of your growing season, your climate, and what you like in a tomato. The varieties you choose should ripen at different times so you can stretch the harvest season. Also, by planting different varieties, you reduce the risk of losing your entire crop to disease. Early season tomatoes don't seem to have as much flavor as the tomatoes that ripen later in the season. So plant just enough of the early tomatoes to get you started, and leave plenty of space for other varieties.

Your neighbors or your local county extension service agent will be the best sources of information on specific tomato varieties that will grow well in your area.

To determine how many tomato plants to grow, figure that each tomato plant will produce about a half bushel, or 30 pounds of tomatoes. That's about 10 quarts of tomatoes per plant. For eating fresh and preserving enough tomatoes for a small family, six to eight tomato plants should be enough.

Tomatoes transplant well, so it is a good idea to start the plants indoors about six to eight weeks before the average last killing frost date.

For starting your tomato plants, choose a container that has holes in the bottom for drainage. Commercial seed flats work well, but you can use any sort of box, pot, or paper cup, as long as there are drainage holes. Fill your container with a sterile potting mix or soil formula. Sprinkle the seeds about ½ inch apart on top of the soil. Pat the seeds down into the soil and cover with a thin layer of soil. Enclose the entire container with a plastic bag to keep in the moisture. Keep the trays in a warm, sunny place. In a few days, the seedlings will appear. Remove the plastic bag. Do not allow the soil to dry out.

When the plants are 3 inches tall, transplant the seedlings into a deeper flat or pot to give the plants more room to grow. Remove all but the uppermost leaves of each plant and bury the plants in soil until only the top leaves show. The tiny "hairs" on the tomato stem will create a strong root system for the plant, and the more roots the plant has, the sturdier and healthier it will be.

When the tomatoes are about 10 inches tall, you can transplant them a second time. Half-gallon milk cartons are ideal for this job. Place the plant in the carton. Pluck off all but the top leaves again, and put soil around the plant so only these top leaves show.

Ten days before you are ready to put your plants in the garden (after the last average frost date), begin to harden off the plants to prepare them for their life in the great outdoors. On the first day, place your plants in a protected area away from wind and sun for a few hours. Each day, lengthen their time outside. After a few days, you can leave the plants outside overnight, unless there is a threat of a frost. It's good to move the plants each day, exposing them to a little more sun and wind with each move.

The last transplanting is to the garden. Dig a trench 5-6 inches deep. Place some seasoned manure or commercial fertilizer in the trench and cover it with 2-3 inches of soil.

If you are planning to stake your tomatoes, put the stakes in now. Carefully remove the tomato plant from its pot and pinch off all but the top leaves. Lay the tomato down in the trench. Cover the remaining stem with 2-3 inches of soil and pat it down firmly. Bring additional soil up around the leaves to prop the leaves in an upright position. Water the plant well. There should be 16-20 inches between the tomato plants.

Once the soil has warmed up, it is a good idea to spread a thick layer of mulch — hay, leaves, straw, even newspapers — around the plants. The best time to mulch is after a heavy rain. The mulch will help the soil retain moisture and will keep the weeds down.

For more information on growing tomatoes, you may want to consult *Down-to-Earth Gardening Know-How for the '90s: Vegetables and Herbs* by Dick Raymond (Storey Publishing).

Now with your tomato plants in the garden and the summer weather promising rich rewards, may all your harvests be bountiful.

TRANSPLANTING TOMATOES

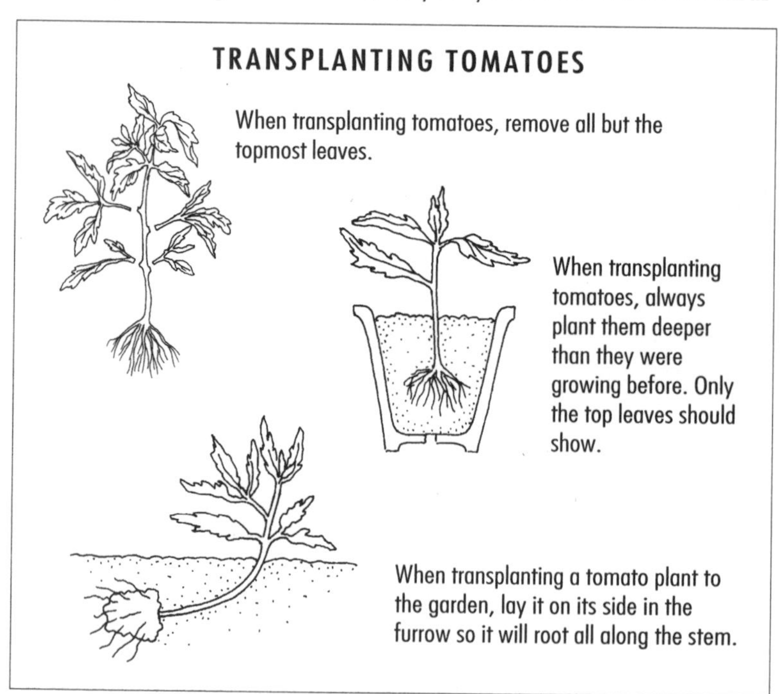

Preserving Tips

There are basically three ways to preserve tomatoes: canning, freezing, and drying. Although producing an excellent end product, canning is quite labor intensive and is difficult to fit into an active lifestyle of work and family responsibilities. This book stresses the use of fresh tomatoes in all the recipes, but you may, of course, substitute any excellent quality, commercially canned tomato product, or if you have the time and inclination, we suggest you contact your local county extension agent for up-to-date home-canning information or consult *Keeping the Harvest* by Nancy Chioffi and Gretchen Mead (Storey Publishing).

FREEZING WHOLE RED TOMATOES

If you have the freezer space, freezing is a good way to preserve tomatoes. You can use frozen tomatoes in any recipe that calls for canned tomatoes.

METHOD ONE:

1. Begin preheating water in a blanching pot.

2. Wash the tomatoes carefully.

3. Place the washed tomatoes in the steamer section of the blanching pot and dip the filled steamer into the boiling water for 30 seconds.

4. Remove the tomatoes to cold water for 1 minute, peel, and quarter.

5. Pack the cooled tomatoes into rigid freezer containers, leaving a 1-inch headspace.

6. Seal and freeze.

METHOD TWO:

1. Wash and core the tomatoes. Do not peel. Set the tomatoes on baking sheets and freeze.

2. When tomatoes are frozen, pack them in plastic freezer bags.

3. If you want to remove the skins before use, defrost the tomatoes first.

FREEZING RED TOMATO SAUCE/PUREE

When using frozen sauces and purees, be sure to defrost the sauce in a bowl and use the liquid that separates from the pulp. It will contain valuable vitamins and should not be thrown away. If you cook the sauce down to a thick consistency, cool the sauce, then freeze it; you will have less liquid separating from the sauce. It is best not to add herbs to sauces before freezing because the herbs often lose flavor or become bitter.

1. Wash fresh tomatoes carefully. Remove blemishes. Cut into quarters.

2. If you have a food mill or strainer that can handle raw tomatoes, process the tomatoes through the food mill or strainer. Otherwise, cook the tomatoes until slightly soft. Cool.

3. Pack the cooled sauce into rigid freezer containers, leaving a 1-inch headspace.

4. Seal and freeze.

DRYING RED TOMATOES

Drying takes very little of your time, although the process will extend over several hours. Most of that time you are free to be elsewhere, while the dehydrator or oven works for you. Use dried tomatoes in soups, stews, sauces, pasta salads, and hot pasta entrées. Also, dried tomatoes can be put into a blender and pulverized into a fine powder, which can be used in dip and soup mixes.

1. Use small to medium-size tomatoes for the best results.

2. Wash the tomatoes carefully. Remove any that are overripe or blemished.

3. The next step is optional: peeling the tomatoes. To do so, place the washed tomatoes in the steamer section of the blancher and immerse in boiling water for 30 seconds. Remove from the boiling water and pour into cold water for 1 minute. Peel and cut out cores. If you plan to make a tomato powder for dip and soup mixes, it is not necessary to peel the tomatoes.

4. Cut the tomatoes into ¼-inch slices, or for sun-dried, cut into quarters. Drain.

5. Dry. In an electric dehydrator, spread the slices on the tray so the pieces do not touch. Dry 8-10 hours at 120° F. until brittle.

For **SUN-DRIED TOMATOES**, spread the quartered tomato pieces on ungalvanized metal screens so that the pieces do not touch. Do not salt the tomato pieces. Cover with cheesecloth to keep off insects. Dry in the hot sun with good air circulation until the tops are dry. Then turn and dry the other sides, until entire product is hard and crisp.

The tomatoes will dry in 1-2 days, if the weather is good. Be sure to bring in the screens at night so the dew will not rehydrate the tomato pieces. See recipes for sun-dried tomatoes on pages 79, 100, 126, and 166.

6. In a **homemade dehydrator or in the oven,** spread the slices on baking sheets so that the pieces do not touch. Dry at 150° F. until the pieces are hard and crisp, turning the slices and rotating the baking sheets once or twice. Store all dried tomatoes in sterile, airtight glass jars in small amounts. Keep away from heat and store the jars in a cool, dark place.

REHYDRATED TOMATOES

If you live in an area with winter temperatures below 40° F., you can have almost-fresh tasting tomatoes for your winter salads. Rehydrate dried tomatoes by spreading the dried tomato quarters on a shallow plate and spraying them with warm water. Let sit for 15 minutes, then spray again. Repeat until the tomato quarters have plumped almost to the thickness of fresh tomatoes. This takes about 1 hour.

PRESERVING PICKLES, RELISHES, JAMS & JELLIES

For equipment, you will need a large water bath canner with rack, specific size canning jars and screw-band lids, and a jar lifter. For more detailed information on preserving these foods, consult *Keeping the Harvest* by Nancy Chioffi and Gretchen Mead (Storey Publishing).

1. Prepare the jars and lids: Wash the jars and check each jar for nicks and cracks — do not use damaged jars. Place the jars in hot water until ready to use and prepare the lids according to manufacturer's directions.

2. Fill the water bath canner half full with hot tap water and begin heating. Invert jars on a towel to drain.

3. Fill the jars with the prepared mixture, following recipe directions.

4. Wipe the jar rims with a clean, damp cloth.

5. Place the lids in position on each jar and tighten the screw bands.

6. Place the jars on the rack in the preheated water bath canner. (The water should not be boiling; if it is, add cold water to cushion the shock of the temperature difference if the jars have cooled slightly.) Lower the jars into the simmering water with a jar lifter. Be careful not to allow the jars to bump against each other. Add boiling water to cover the jars by 2 inches. (Do *not* pour boiling water directly on jars.) Cover the canner and bring the water to a boil.

7. Begin counting processing time when the water in the canner has started a rapid boil.

8. When the processing time is completed, remove the jars with the jar lifter and place on heavy towels away from drafts. Allow to cool for 12-24 hours.

9. When the jars are cool, remove the screw bands and test the seals. A jar is sealed when the lid is depressed in the center. Wipe the jars clean and store sealed jars in a cool, dark place. If improperly sealed, use the preserve immediately, or recan. To recan, repack the preserve in a clean, sterilized jar with a *new*, clean, sterilized lid and reprocess.

IMPORTANT RULES FOR SUCCESS

- Use **only** firm, unbruised food.
- Arrange all equipment beforehand and thoroughly clean work area.
- Use **only** standard jars and lids intended for home preserving. Follow the manufacturer's directions for sealing the jars.
- Label and date the preserved food.

KEEPING GREEN TOMATOES

After trying some of the recipes for green tomatoes, you will probably consider harvesting green tomatoes, way before the first frost if you live in a cold climate. But when that first frost does hit, if you have many green tomatoes still on the vine, you will be faced with a big storage problem. Nevertheless, try to avoid frost damage by covering the tomatoes with heavy cloths when you get a frost warning.

SORTING GREEN TOMATOES

Harvest green tomatoes and sort by degree of ripeness. Place the tomatoes in cardboard boxes, cover with newspapers, and store in a cool, dark place. The warmer the tomatoes are, the sooner they will ripen. At 65-70° F., mature green tomatoes will ripen in about two weeks. At 55° F., they will ripen in about four weeks. Be sure you check the tomatoes frequently and remove ripe ones and any that are beginning to spoil.

FREEZING GREEN TOMATOES

Use frozen green tomatoes in any recipe calling for heated and cooked ingredients. If you want to remove the skins before use, defrost the tomatoes first. Frozen slices may be dipped in flour and fried in hot vegetable oil without thawing.

1. Wash and core the tomatoes. Do not peel.

2. Cut the tomatoes into ¼-inch slices or ½-inch cubes and spread them in a single layer on baking sheets. Freeze.

3. When the tomatoes are frozen, pack them in plastic freezer bags.

DRYING GREEN TOMATOES

After soaking dried green tomatoes for one hour in an equal amount of water, you can use them in any recipe calling for chopped green tomatoes.

1. Wash, core, and peel the tomatoes.

2. Cut the tomatoes into ½-inch cubes. Drain.

3. Follow Step 5 in the section Drying Red Tomatoes on page 275, using either a dehydrator, oven, or the sun.

4. Follow Step 6 in the section Drying Red Tomatoes on page 276.

FREEZING GREEN TOMATO PUREE

As you have seen in chapters 3 and 4, there are many delicious ways to cook with green tomatoes. So, it is a good idea to freeze some green tomato puree to use in soups, sauces, and desserts.

1. Wash 10 pounds of green tomatoes. Dice.

2. Combine the tomatoes in a large saucepan with 2 cups water and ¼ cup honey. Simmer for 15 minutes, or until the tomatoes are very soft. Blend until smooth. Cool.

3. Pack the cooled puree into rigid freezer containers in 1-cup batches.

4. Seal and freeze.

Preparing Tips

To peel tomatoes, bring a medium-size saucepan of water to a boil. Wash and core the tomatoes. Drop the tomatoes, one or two at a time, into the boiling water for 15 seconds. Remove with a slotted spoon and cool under cold water. The tomato skin will easily peel or even fall off.

Remove excess liquid and seeds from tomatoes by cutting them in half horizontally and gently squeezing and shaking out the liquid.

If you have **leftover tomato paste** after preparing a meal, flash freeze it in small amounts to use later in sauces, soups, or stews. Line a baking sheet with wax paper and put dollops of tomato paste (about 1 tablespoon each) on the sheet. Freeze uncovered until firm. Transfer the frozen tomato paste into sealable, plastic freezer bags and store in the freezer.

1 POUND TOMATOES =
2 large tomatoes
3 medium tomatoes
4 small tomatoes

2 CUPS CHOPPED TOMATOES =
1½ pounds

1 QUART CHOPPED TOMATOES =
5 large tomatoes
7 medium tomatoes
8-10 small tomatoes

28-OUNCE COMMERCIALLY CANNED TOMATOES =
6 large tomatoes
3 cups chopped tomatoes

INDEX